SEQUELLAND

A STORY OF DREAMS AND SCREAMS

JAY SLAYTON-JOSLIN

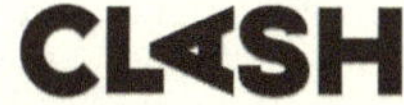

Cover by Matthew Revert

ISBN: 978-1-944866-71-6

CLASH Books

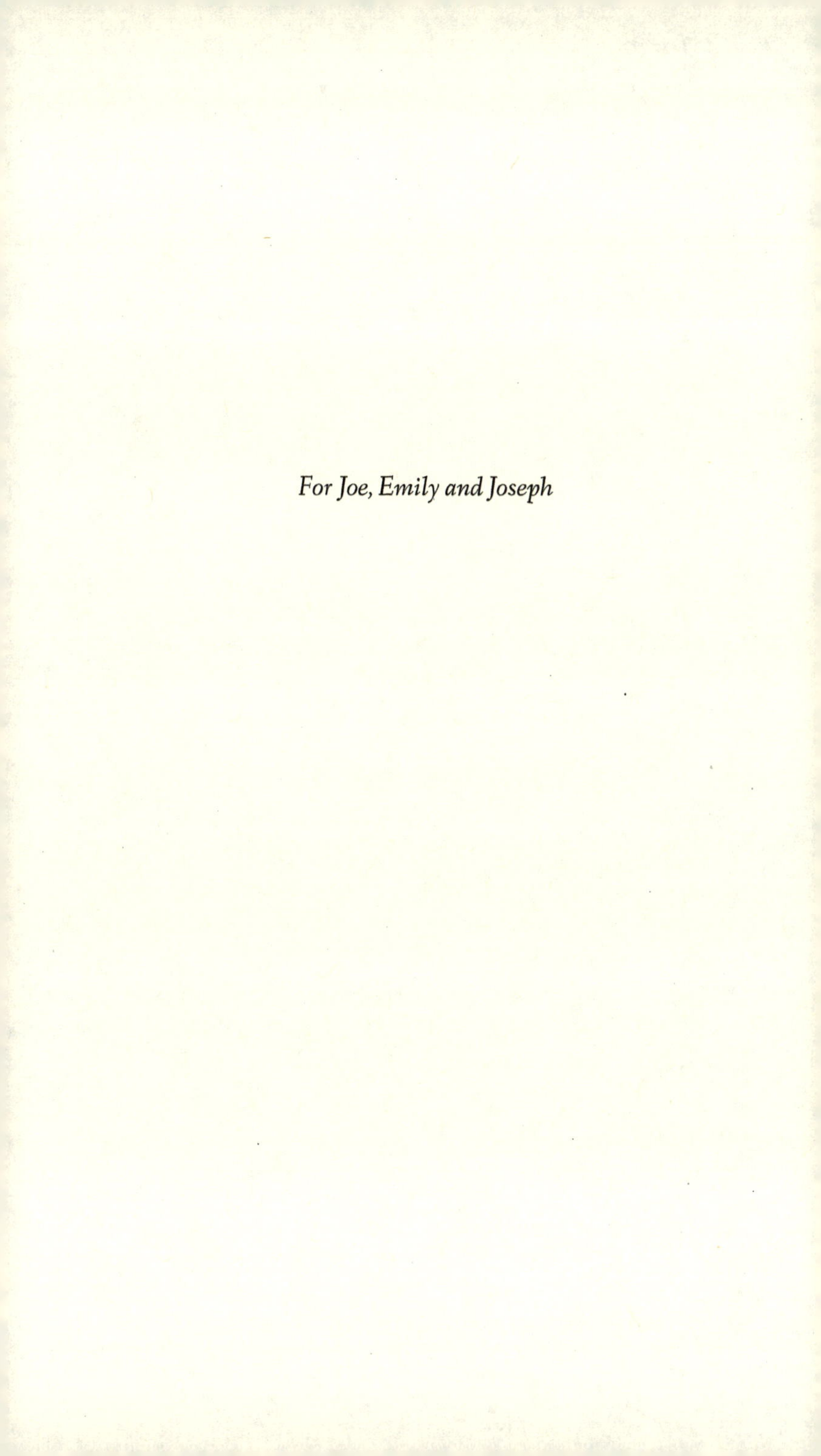

For Joe, Emily and Joseph

CONTENTS

Introduction vii

SET UP 1
Interview with Kevin Greutert 7
Interview with Katt Shea 15
FIRST INCITING INCIDENT 21
Interview with Zach Lipovsky 27
Interview with Uwe Boll 33
DEVELOPMENT 49
Interview with Kevin Yagher 55
Interview with Mary Lambert 61
Interview with Peter Webber 63
SECOND INCITING INCIDENT 71
Interview Ernie Barbarash 77
Interview Adam Marcus 91
CLIMAX 117
Interview with Jeff Burr 121
Interview with John Skipp 137
RESOLUTION 145
FADE OUT 151

Acknowledgments 153
About the Author 155
ALSO BY CLASH BOOKS 157

INTRODUCTION

I've never stopped worrying about what's in the shadows. I keep the blinds closed because I think there may be someone out there in a mask creeping up on me. I wonder about finding bodies in abandoned buildings and am glad my bed has storage underneath so monsters can't hide there.

I grew up on horror movies. Boxsets of *Nightmare on Elm Street* for Christmas, raiding the family DVDs for anything with an 18 + rating and gore—I wanted to be scared and to have nightmares. I think being a writer encourages you to go to those unknown places, to live in your brain and more often than not that can be a terrifying place. You constantly wonder about things that could happen to others, yourself, and how that can change the world as you know it.

I haven't written any horror stories, or at least not in the conventional way. Nothing about burial grounds, no wendigos or cannibals; the only thing going bump in the night in my stories was my protagonist stumbling home from a drunk. In reality, I'm constantly scared by how the world is unfolding and how powerless we are to do anything about it. It's part of why I tend to write about depressed nothingness and people who have the choice to change but continue to be a shitty person, because those scenarios are far more realistic to me than anything taking over the world.

I have notebooks with outlines of serial killers that are inspired by urban legends, of families who move to a neighbourhood where they're not welcome and cults that specifically target the protagonist. If, or more accurately, when I write one of these—the idea that it could be boring or not at all scary is enough to cripple me each time I sit down at my laptop.

With horror, it feels like that much more of a holy ground because it's something I consume that I love and perhaps it would be tainted for me if I can't create something I love. Though, as I type this, I know that it doesn't mean that I won't try, out of respect for myself and all the countless films, games and paperbacks I've torn through over the years. It's the lore and the continuous story that's stuck with me over the years.

The way a series of novels can detail a character or a whole universe, I've found that same magic in horror films and their sequels. Whether it's an actor reprising their role after 20 years, or a throwaway sentence about them being away because the actor wouldn't come back—all of it adds something to the world.

The kid in me can't get enough of the gore. I love the storytelling, the blood, and the familiar thrills a horror franchise can consistently deliver. Plus, there's so many of them. The digital age has robbed me of the pleasure of scanning every DVD in an old shop, rubbing my fingers against the spines and looking at the cover art to see which might be the scariest, as I sit crossed legged on the aisle floor. For older folks, this may be replicated with a cult section and VHS. I hope in the streaming age we get something similar to the Direct to DVD Sequels, because, man did they make me happy.

It's because of the pure joy they brought me that I want to look at those sequels and understand how they work — or, if they didn't, why not. They say if you don't learn from history you're doomed to repeat it, and while I'm no bastion of perfect art, perhaps I can extend that to mean if we can learn from previous artists, we can learn how to not make the same mistakes ourselves and recognise when it's going right. Plus, y'know, there might be some cool stories from our favourite franchises, I'm not going to say it's purely some altruistic quest here.

Everyone in this book has a passion for what they do, it takes some crazy kind of drive to see a piece of art and run at it to make it better. Sometimes it is just a job, but more often than not it's a labour of love. Sometimes that love can pay the bills, sometimes it can leave you never wanting to look back on it. Sometimes we have to look into the shadows of anothers' art to see the work that lives in ourselves.

SET UP

For most of my life I've been that kid that stares out the classroom window, thinking about the movie that I saw the night before, the book I was reading, the video game where I made the choices that influenced the story.

For me it was never enough to be content at the end of the film, particularly in horror, where there tends to be a last minute closeup of the slasher as their eyes open, implying they've got another blood bath in them. Stephen King famously talks about the *what if?* And when we look back at franchises these questions tend to be answered for us rather than allowing the viewer to develop it themselves: What if Michael Myers wanted revenge after being shot and would never give up? What if escaping Leatherface didn't stop the cannibal family? What if a teen girl with psychic powers wasn't an isolated incident? What if making sequels to great films was more of a cash grab by studios, and that it is only because of fans and directors who love these movies that we get to expand on the originals that brought us nightmares? I know these questions because I've asked them hundreds of times myself.

As a writer, I know that the deeper you delve into being a creator, the process and what that actually means, the more complicated it gets. When my first book came out, a little poetry collection called *Kicking Prose*, I was thrilled. I would carry several copies of it everywhere, like I was allergic to oxygen and it was my EpiPen.

Looking back on it now, coming up to six years since its release, I'm indifferent to how I feel about it. It's the best that I could do at that time, and I can do better now – though I suppose that is the right way round. It's probably harder for the directors featured in this book than it was for me, not just because they had to work with more people than I have—small presses are usually one or two people and a cover artist, if that—but they were brought in when something had already been created. They were writing and creating the sequel to something that most of them were not involved in.

In this book, there are creators who began their careers with a sequel and never even directed again. For others, it was the beginning of a long career, and for some, it was a step down after having already achieved fame and success. Some worked as hard as they could and then went on to other projects, others never left the project and the reputation from it behind. It's difficult to say why these directors got involved with established franchises in the way that they did, and even looking back on the whole collection now, I'm not a lot closer to getting an answer that isn't vague, but I am closer. If you were given the choice to do something that wasn't going to be a nightmare of studio executives

making decisions, in your dream field, to do something with the material that inspired you, would you take the job? I would. I don't like the answer to that question from an originality and creative standpoint, but to get paid to do what I love, to be able to say yes to all those previous things? It beats my 9-5. It's not as if the height of my artistic ambitions is to write *Slaughterhouse-Six* but it doesn't mean that in the right circumstances it wouldn't be tempting, either.

Perhaps that's the real reason I'm doing this: tracking down people who made movies decades ago, because it's really just a way to understand the creator, something that I am and forever hope to be. Perhaps one day there will be someone trying to ask me some questions. Me, the boy who helped his mother decorate the Christmas tree while *The Exorcist* was playing in the background, the boy who talks about the difference of quality in the *Wrong Turn* movies repeatedly to his close friends, the boy who perhaps prefers the secrets of fictional worlds than the truth of real ones.

I think there's great comfort in a franchise, it's the same reason that people fall in love with characters over the seasons of a TV show, compared to a standalone single entry, there's room to grow. You're rewarded for the nerdiest references and characters that you recognise, and just because there's blood and guts in a film does not mean there isn't love. Sometimes it's the universe that is more exciting, even when it's our own. In *Texas Chainsaw Massacre,* Leatherface certainly is terrifying in his clumsiness as well as his chainsaw, but the fact that his killing multiple people doesn't make him the most horrifying member in the cannibal Sawyer family speaks volumes.

Did you know that the first sequel was *The Fall of a Nation*? If you're thinking that this sounds uncomfortably similar to the KKK favourite, *The Rise of A Nation,* then you're absolutely justified, as it's a sequel. It wasn't successful at all and the production company went bankrupt having only made this film, and the film is now considered lost. I think there is some irony that for so long in the film industry, over a century, there have been attempts to cash grab and go back with something that executives think the audience wants. Even though in the future this will be seen as the years when Disney dominated the cinemas, there are notable failures. For every *Avengers Infinity War* there's a *Solo*. The strength in horror comes from the *Paranormal Activities* and *Blair Witch Projects*, the ambitious films made on a budget so low it wouldn't serve as a deposit for a house in L.A. It's this creativity that comes from so little that is truly inspiring, and more than likely to be monopolised upon, too.

I feel like creating is often a love story. There is something that we want to express, and the form that it can take feels like so many different things that sometimes the ambition and desire to tell it the way we see it in our head makes us want to explode. It's easy to go in as critics, reviewers, or just audience members, and understand the backstory behind the creation. This doesn't excuse it from being bad, but just that there is more than one level to consider. It feels like an indecisive point to make, but one that should be made regardless. Perhaps it's me saving my own skin, perhaps you'll close the pages of the book and forgive me for my mistakes and understand what I was trying to create. Hopefully you'll understand the area where I'm coming from, because I believe in subcultures there are not just regular truths, but pure humane truths because it's people expressing themselves from a vulnerable place.

I want to tell you a secret: despite this being a book about horror, artists, creating and a career in retrospective, it's actually a book about me and you. It's a book about the people who when they lay down at night and look up at the stars, they don't think about what is out there, but about parasites on a meteor coming to infest us and how we would fight back, the kind of people who have their zombie escape plan to go to, the people that know that if a curse is placed on them and they are being chased by a killer with a knife, how they'll survive and fight back. It's a way for people to understand the things that they love by learning about those that created them and why, a chance for people to learn about themselves, too.

INTERVIEW WITH KEVIN GREUTERT

"Why couldn't you make that decision BEFORE we finished the movie?"

Selected Filmography:

Saw VI
Saw 3D
Jessabelle
Visions
Jackal

What began your interest in film making, how did you get started?

Like many people, I've been fascinated by films since I first started watching them. And also like many people, I didn't have much of an idea of how movies came to exist, at least not when I was a little kid. But I started to put the pieces together watching Godzilla-type movies. It would seem that it is some people's JOB to build intricate models of cities, then put on monster costumes and SMASH THE MODELS TO PIECES. Why would you ever want to do anything else? I got a still camera in 3rd grade and started to set up dioramas of destruction using army men toys and dinosaur models. Would love to make a movie now using miniatures, but the thing that got me first interested in movies just doesn't happen much anymore. Everything is C.G.

I fantasized a lot about being a writer when I was a kid. This might have been a more realistic pursuit, since I don't really have what you might call a "director's personality", I'm more introverted than otherwise. But I have always been very attracted to the notion of creating new realities, which is what film making is.

You started on the *Saw* films as an editor, what was it like seeing the franchise grow and expand exponentially?

It was really fun to be part of the series. We worked really hard on those movies, and tried hard to never be boring. Sometimes I'm working on other stuff, and it'll strike me that something lazy is happening, that we're a little bit asleep at the wheel, making assumptions about how engaged the audience should be at a given point in the story, and I'll remember how tightly we tried to cut the *Saws*, especially the first two. It was mind blowing to see the *Saw* movies take off like they did, felt pretty surreal at the time. Really great to see James' career take off like it did, and still getting bigger with each project.

As the franchise grew, how difficult was it to manage the lore and story that evolved?

Because you see a film hundreds of times in the course of editing it, I had a really strong handle on every detail of the storyline. That said, I didn't have much influence on the script until *Saw VI,* but I worked closely with the directors on the films leading up to that, so I did what I could to keep it as clear as possible. After *Saw VI,* particularly *Jigsaw,* I didn't really have much influence on the story at all.

What led to you being chosen as the director of *Saw VI* and *Final Chapter?*

I had been nudging the producers to let me direct starting with *Saw III*. At that time, Darren was planning on doing something else, but they eventually wrangled him back to direct *IV* in exchange for producing *Repo the Genetic Opera* for him. I had moved on to edit *The Strangers* instead of *Saw IV,* but when Darren decided to return to the franchise, he talked me into finishing *IV* when I was done with *Strangers*. The producers liked what I did enough to offer me a lot of dough to edit *Saw V* and VI, to be directed by David Hackl. I decided to decline and pursue other avenues. Then they came back and said if I edited *Saw V*, they'd let me direct *Saw V*I. So that's how that happened, by playing hardball.

Final Chapter was a lot different. After *VI*, I got offered to make *Paranormal Activity* 2, and got to an advanced stage with the script treatment. But I had to go back to the *Saw* producers and get permission to do a film outside the *Saw* franchise, because they had a one year option on my next film. They didn't want me to do *Paranormal*, so they exercised the option, and in less than a week I was back in Toronto and hurled into production. Ugh, those were rough times.

At the time was the *Final Chapter* truly believed to be the final piece of the *Saw* franchise, and if

so, did this make it difficult & challenging to direct and deliver to the fans?

I tried to convince the producers to let me make *Saw VI* be the final chapter! Hoffman would have died at the end, and we would have sold it as the last one. They refused. I tried again when we made *Saw VII*, and they still refused to make it the last one. We literally finished the movie before they changed their minds and decided to change the title to *The Final Chapter*. Before that, the title was "Saw 3D: The Traps Come Alive", which is second only to *Haunting in Connecticut 2: Ghosts of Georgia* for true terribleness. At the time, I was like, Wait – we didn't MAKE this to be the final chapter, why couldn't you make that decision BEFORE we finished the movie? Yeah, that was pretty rough too. Now *Jigsaw* is panting to restart the franchise, but who knows if it will lead to another one. I know they're keen to keep going, but it's pretty tough considering John Kramer died in *Saw III*.

Why did you not return to direct *Jigsaw*?

They didn't ask me. The studio wanted "fresh blood", a new stylistic take on the series. I was a little reluctant to come back as editor, but they were generous and I had a pretty good time, so it was fine. Maybe a future instalment...

With the *Saw* films being so iconic, how do you foresee the franchise going in the future?

Hard to tell. Everyone involved wants to keep Tobin Bell in the story, but it's just getting so hard to do. The producers wisely don't want to go in a supernatural or science fiction direction to bring Jigsaw back to life, but it would clearly be risky to just drop him from the storyline because he really is the face of the franchise. But it's sooooo hard to find relevant ways to keep telling his story. It's made pretty clear in *Saw*

III and *IV* that Kramer only became a serial killer at the end of his life, so it's not like you can easily tell a story that takes place before *Saw 1*.

Whilst being known for your work in the *Saw* films, has it been challenging or refreshing to pursue work outside of this franchise?

I have embraced making films that are very different than *Saw*, but it's a lot harder to get recognition for them! By the time I directed *Saw VI*, it was a very famous franchise. My other films have been low budget and stand alone, so I'm always starting from scratch, and thus far have yet to get much traction. But I'll keep trying as long as people hire me!

What other films would you like to make across your career?

I just wrote a South Pacific adventure story I'd love to make. I've written a romantic comedy about a Russian spy in the Cold War, a romantic comedy about digital personal assistants, a supernatural thriller about contacting the dead, and am currently writing another haunted house story. I'm very attracted to science fiction, but haven't been able to shoot one yet.

One thing I'm curious about, if you don't mind discussing, is how the critical reception of the *Saw* films influenced production, studios and the general creation over time. Some of the sequels were loved by fans, so I'm just interested as to whether you think this is down to how critics perceive horror films, or if it's nothing of interest to the studio nor does it have an impact on your career?

From the beginning, I tracked the fan response on forums such as House of Jigsaw, IMDB, and tried to keep a finger on what was working with the audience and what wasn't. The critical response was always bad, even for the first *Saw*, which is now considered a horror classic. My tastes tended to be strongly in line with the audience in terms of the characters who spoke to me or didn't, so for example I petitioned strongly to bring Shawnee Smith and Cary Else back to the story, which was very hard to do.

The role that the producers took in developing the storyline was more based on their instincts regarding what was working and what wasn't. One of them was very surprised when some fans at an event told them that *Saw VI* was their favorite (he thought *V* was the best). This may have played a part in their decision to bring me back for *Saw VII*, though by that time the script was already written and most of the sets were built. Developing the storylines was always a vigorous back and forth between the producers and the writers/directors. Nothing unusual about that I suppose.

The studio was most active in making sure the franchise included "branding" elements they could use to market the film, such as "I want to play a game", the pig mask, insistence on keeping Tobin's face in the movies. They do lots of market research, though it's rare that they share the raw data with the film makers; we mostly get it through marching orders about these iconic elements. Most horror movies that make a lot of money don't get good critical reviews, except for some very rare "respectable" movies like *The Conjuring*. There are of course indie darlings like *It Follows* and *The Babadook* that don't necessarily make a lot of money and don't get wide releases, but they can launch careers. So, I think there's a lot more studio traffic on Box Office Mojo than Rotten Tomatoes when it comes to guessing their thinking.

How does it feel to know you've contributed to

one of the most famous post 2000 film franchises?

Saw came to me out of left field, while I was an assistant editor on Disney movies. It changed my life, and really made my career, opened so many doors and introduced me to so many people. For something so hellish and dark and blood-smeared, it has been an angel from Heaven for me!

INTERVIEW WITH KATT SHEA

"We didn't actually think they would do it without us – but they did."

Selected Filmography:

Stripped To Kill
Stripped To Kill II: Live Girls
Poison Ivy
The Rage: Carrie 2

Let's start by talking about the *Poison Ivy*

Well I had nothing to do with the sequels.

I mean the whole idea of somebody else getting involved on the world you did on the franchise. It was quite a popular film; how did you get started on the project?

Andy Ruben and I met with the producers. It was based on Lauren Blyth, an experience she had when she was young. The reason they wanted to do it was because of the movie Andy and I did together call *Streets* staring Christina Applegate.

Did you have a big input on the writing of the screenplay?

Andy was the writer and I was the director. We had written a number of movies together that were produced. There was *Stripped To Kill, Stripped To Kill II, Dance of the Dammed, Streets*. We had done that and then we did *Poison Ivy*.

A good working relationship?

Yep.

Were you given notice when the sequels were produced?

Well, yeah, they asked us if we wanted to do *Poison Ivy II*, and it seemed like such a crazy idea because Ivy dies at the end. To us, it seemed like just an idea to make more money. They didn't expect it to be as successful as it was and they wanted more money. The trend stemmed from that. We didn't actually think they would do it without us – but they did.

Did you see the movie?

No. I've heard some pretty negative things and never saw it. They didn't care. They exploited it completely, it's not something I really wanted to see.

And I presume it was the same for the other two sequels as well?

Yeah. I think it's contaminated – the whole essence of what *Poison Ivy* was, it's pretty sad. I'm sad about it, why do they have to do it that way? They could have been more ambitious about what they were doing, keeping up the quality.

They weren't worrying about that. They were just after a fast buck.

Do you know why they decided to make a fourth sequel so late?

I'm sure it's just motivated by money. That was the only motivation to the sequels. I'm sure the director had higher aspirations, it's just hard when the studio itself only cares about exploiting it.

And then there was *The Rage: Carrie 2*. How did you get involved?

Another director was already directing it. The studio was going to fire it and scrap the movie, and rather than do that they brought me in. Because of my reputation of low budget and making high quality products for that budget. They were already two weeks into shooting and they needed to save the money and stay on budget. I had to throw away two weeks of work and stay on budget with what they had.

Was most of the budget spent in those two weeks?

I was left with enough. The film is all there. It makes it a bit of a challenge, but I like a challenge. I'm very grateful for the opportunity to have made that movie. I'm grateful for the opportunity for *Poison Ivy*. I don't mean to slam New Line, they gave us a lot of creative freedom to make the film we wanted to make. So I have to really applaud New Line for that. It's what they did afterwards that made me so sad. Here they had a film that opened at MoMa in New York and was critically acclaimed, and they made sex movies out of that – it doesn't make any sense why. Taking something that really had a lot of cache to it and throwing it down the toilet. It doesn't make sense to me. But I'm grateful I had the opportunity to make that.

Did you see the original *Carrie* movie?

Of course, when I was a kid. It was so profound. It's an amazing film, one of my favourite of all time. It was an honour to come in after that and really scary – how do you follow that? You can't. You really can't.

Where you aware of that when directing, you couldn't match?

Of course, when they asked me to do it I was like oh my god how do you do this. Coming up to Brian Palmer and Stephen King? You can't match it in any way. The original is one of the truly great films of all time. It resonated with me so strongly as a kid.

Stephen King has had some great adaptations.

His work lends itself to being filmed.

Did you have any dialogue with Stephen King?

No, I did with Brian De Palma but not Stephen King. I didn't write *Carrie* 2. I wrote all my other films with Andy Ruben, I was hired on a Thursday and flew in to North Carolina and started shooting on Monday. There's parts of North Carolina that looks like the East Coast. At first I was sceptical, and they saved a lot of money, but when I got there, I was there recently and it's gorgeous, just reminds me of the East Coast so much.

Did you see the 2002 or 2013 *Carrie* films?

I didn't.

Did you not want to ruin the perception of the original?

I heard some not so great things. I don't watch a lot of films, I'm not the kind of cinephile that watches every film that comes out. I really watch very few films. I think I only watch really good films that people talk about in a positive way. I don't mean critics; I mean real movie viewers. That's what makes me interested, not movie reviews.

What films have you enjoyed recently?

I really shouldn't do interviews, though I'm known for horror movies I watch comedy. I'm a big Judd Apatow film fan. I just started to watch his movies this year. I saw *Love and Mercy* which was good, *Straight Outta Compton* which was a bit sugar coated but it was fun to watch. Saying these were just good boys doing gangster rap. I don't believe that was really the case, but I'm not an expert, I just find it hard to believe.

What made you decide to open an acting school?

When I did *Stripped To Kill* I cast real strippers in it and hosted acting classes in my living room. I like working with actors and helping them get to the highest potential they have and I have a really good way of doing that.

You've worked with amazing actors.

Yeah, it comes naturally to me to help actors. I think it's because I'm not a good actor. Really good actors can't teach because they've got it. I understand the pitfalls and the things that stop you and I know how to get around those things and that's made me a really good teacher and I love teaching so I keep doing it.

Do you have future directing plans?

I was supposed to be directing a movie now, but I think it's fallen through, though I don't know for sure. I'm sure I'll direct something in the next four years, if not this project something else.

Do you prefer teaching?

Yes. Quite simply, yes. It's none of the drama. So much of the ego, people with agendas and a lot of money and people get really weird when they have money riding on things. It's just very very challenging to direct and do it well with all the different agendas going on.

FIRST INCITING INCIDENT

When you're starting out, especially when you're young, it's hard to know what you want to say. It's something that even now I struggle with, as who I am each year of my life, each day I sit down at the keyboard, changes completely. When I started writing it was very much copying the style of writers that I admired at the time. I was so focused on figuring out how to say something that it almost didn't really matter what I was saying, just that it mimics the transgressive authors I read. Part of that still stays with me, because knowing that there is an artist out there who understands you means you're less lonely, and as we grow in this day of social media and instant interaction and supposed gratification, it's easier to feel lonely when we're connected to billions.

My book *Kicking Prose* was a collection of sad poems about girls and growing up and not knowing how, it is about how we are falling apart and making it seem like we have it together. This book, I think, is a continuation of that theme – how through everything as creators, we continue and create. Much like the audience who root for the characters to run away from the villains, I'll always root for an under-dog. I'm probably the least objective person who can look at my own work, but I think this shows continually. I think there is a dangerous lack of self-awareness when you're young. I think when we start creating, we dream of how we are going to change the world, and not the level of work it takes to do it.

I remember planning a novel called *This is Eighteen*, that was meant to sum up the coming of age experience I was waiting to happen. It didn't matter to me that the only novel I had ever come close to finishing was a first draft of a Young Adult post-apocalyptic novel for NaNoWriMo that I never bothered spellchecking or taking out the song lyrics I included because I wanted to hit my word count easier. I just felt that I could do it. It took me years to realise that creating a piece of art is like building a muscle, you need to work hard and build at it regularly if you want to get stronger. Of course, there are many literary masterpieces that can be seen as exceptions to this rule, but if we always hold ourselves to exceptions then we never get to build a foundation to create on.

The directors I interviewed for this book worked mercilessly at what they cared about before getting their shot. If you look at Adam Marcus, his first directorial feature was working on a Jason Voorhees film, but there's clearly a long history of him cutting his teeth in the industry. It shows that despite some Rotten Tomatoes ratings. These are hard working and talented people that from a young age decided what they were going to focus on and made it happen.

Realistically, this is the moment in people's lives that separates the doers from dreamers, from the guy that always talks about making a film to the one that decides to write a script and grab a camera. Success is more complicated than this, opportunistic and down to luck, so it's not to discredit the people that never make it, as there are plenty of them out there, and at this stage I am one of those people, but at least they tried. I respect someone who sets out their goals and goes for them a million times unsuccessfully more than an infinite number of attempts at get rich quick schemes.

With age and ambition there are innumerable benefits to having someone you can go to with your work, that serves as a mentor. This person can take many forms: a friend, an executive producer, editor or any other role that teaches and enables you. It comes from the realisation that you are setting out on a journey and it is difficult but someone can help show you the way and keep you on the path. It's this moment of realisation, the respect for yourself, others and your art that is one of the biggest developments anyone can have. It's like being in a restaurant and waiting for your food to arrive, you rarely leave it an exact amount before you get impatient, but like a light switch you realise that it's taking too long. It's with this sudden realisation that you have the idea of what you should be doing and how, and for what reason.

For me, I know one of the biggest realisations came after years of writing. Years of seeing submission calls and great opportunities at presses where I would write something and send in pitches for things that I didn't really consider myself a good fit for, just so that there was a chance of a publication or a deal. Sometimes these things work and you can get paid or create something good because things come out of your comfort zone, but the ability to understand what you're about and what you want to do is so much more liberating than chasing the end goal.

It's easier to talk about this from my experience of sending short stories to publishers and pretending I had a collection because I know exactly what I've worked on that has come to fruition, but do not forget that the directors in this book have had multiple meetings and passion projects, possibly just missing out on jobs that were critically acclaimed and that behind every IMDB score is a story as well.

The relationship between the artist and their art is no different to any kind of relationship. It can be a quick encounter that can be finished in a night, something that consumes us across months and years, even if it doesn't ultimately work out. Very few people work at a passion that is more likely to disappoint them financially and socially than reward them, so there's only the understanding that it's the creation and end goal of the art itself is what drives us forward.

If you're anything like me, you can find it tedious, and after a day at work or going to the gym, sometimes the last thing I want to do is sit down at the keyboard, getting into the habit of typing words and hitting the space bar like I'm learning to play the bass and having to get my computer repaired, rather than just playing video games and having a drink. That being said, if you're like me, you'll understand that in games, movies and books there are moment that makes it all worth it. These are the moments that for us give our lives purpose, that make it seem better while we worry about things in our day to day life because someone else understands that too, and that's why they create. I realised quickly that I wouldn't become a director, but that doesn't mean that some of the films, ones made by directors in this book didn't give me the same awe when I was growing up.

Each of these directors have moments where they realised this was their passion as well as their job. Sometimes one of those two overpowers the over when we need to pay bills, or focus on what we really want to do. Some of these stories are shared in this book; the moment where they stared at the screen and someone inspired something for them, others aren't, and that's fine because it is an intimate moment to share with someone. What incites the desire to create is different for everyone, and in these horror films there is surely a new generation of people that want to direct movies, and that's an accomplishment to bring that energy into the world that not many people can say they've achieved.

We have to understand that discussing art as well as creating it is just as important as supporting it, there are billions of people in the world whose stories have not been told, and even if they never will be, if we can create something that they can cling onto and gives them that bit of hope, then that is successful. Of course, art can take so many different turns and invoke so many different reactions, but the story of this book is one of those who were inspired to create as some had before them, and how they may influence those that come after.

INTERVIEW WITH ZACH LIPOVSKY

"Each film I've made has been a step closer to what I want to do."

Selected Filmography:

Tasmanian Devils
Leprechaun: Origins
Dead Rising: Watchtower

What made you get started in film making?

I started as an actor, my mum was a television producer for children's programming and I was cheap free talent. When I was 7, I got an agent and did it for other people and was a big computer nerd and made my own movie with digital effects and learned how to make my own stuff while on sets. By the time I was in high school I was volunteering a lot in lots of indie stuff and after high school my mum said "I would have supported you for university, so I'll support you into film making." I volunteered on every set I could and did digital effects for every film I could. By the time I started directing I had years of favours to call upon—and then I was off to the races.

And, an extra bonus, you got to be in the *Goosebumps* TV series?

Actually at the time I was in grade 4 – 9 or 10 – and everyone was reading *Goosebumps* at the time. That was the first big show I was in, it was so amazing. I think I got a cheque for $30 last week for that.

Was it weird being on the other side of the camera?

No because I was always making my own movies. I enjoyed it more anyway. Acting was always just a fun side-track, and a great way of getting out of school.

How did you get involved in the *Leprechaun* franchise?

That was already getting made. I didn't originate it. Basically, WWE and Lionsgate decided to have a partnership and looked at the franchises they had between them and decided that *Leprechaun* would be a good one to reboot. They wanted to shoot it in Vancouver, and to get the tax credit they had to hire a Canadian. Americans often want to hire Canadians for a tax break, but don't know anybody. I made a monster movie before that. I made a film before that in the same country, same genre same budget, almost same plot. They needed someone quickly. Basically, my agent called me up at like 9 in the morning and said I'm sending you a script. And by 2pm I was in the meeting. By the end of the meeting they said can you be in Vancouver on Monday and I said yes and I was on the plane.

Were you familiar with the franchise before?

I was familiar, but not a diehard fan. Mostly the first film and what Warwick Davis had done and what the franchise represented. It was unique as a slapstick horror comedy, which wasn't mine or the Studio's franchise. A film at the time that had just been rebooted was *Evil Dead* that had a much grittier and darker reboot, *Dark Knight* style. So then they wanted to do something similar. Which was where my interest was, we were never going to duplicate what the original films were going to do. They nailed that and didn't need it to be done again, we weren't going to replicate that and see what else we can do. And see what kind of scary movie you can make with something as silly as a leprechaun—that was the challenge for me.

Since you were doing a reboot, was it nice not worrying about continuity?

I was more aware of it than the studio and distributors were. I tried to put as many homages as possible in there, which gave me a lot of freedom. It's been split two ways as far as reception. People who loved the original series hate it, fair enough, and people who don't know the original franchise like it. So I think that's totally fair. I had a lot less control over that film. I was just trying to make the best film I could with the material I was given.

Did it succeed in spawning a new franchise?

I know it did financially well. I don't know if they're racing to make ten more of them. I know it succeeded in helping sell a lot more of the franchise because they released the original box set with the new one, so I think that probably generated a lot of money.

It's not like you're in a meeting to do another one?

No, and I probably wouldn't do it either.

When people mention the *Leprechaun* franchise do you have a conscious association with the franchise or just view it as a job?

No, in my head it was a clean start. The studios were very clear that they wanted almost nothing to do with the originals, and I think that might have hurt them. They were so afraid of the originals that they pulled back in ways that hurt the film. I see them as two separate things, which is bizarre when you're doing a reboot, but that's what the project was. They were so afraid of it being silly that they shied away from things I thought would have been cool and terrifying. I feel that when you do a horror film you have to really go for it and be risky, otherwise the horror film won't make an impact, because that's what the genre is. In my mind, I don't see them as connected.

Did you want to go into horror?

My love is for action adventure. Spielbergian 80s movies, that sense of wonder is my love. All the films I have made have been horror movies. You can either start in comedy, drama or horror, those are the three schools you can start climbing the ladders in. While I like it and like a lot of horror films, still has a lot of the tools that play into action adventure: set up pay off, sequence, lighting and styling. All the things I love are present in horror. The horror films I've done end up being adventure films, like in *Leprechaun* when they're huddled up around the map, it felt to me like a scene from *The Goonies*, they've all got lanterns learning about this mystical world. Each film I've made has been a step closer to what I want to do.

And *Dead Rising: Watchtower* was a prime example of that.

Dead Rising was given a lot more freedom to make it my own. It is more an action film that has zombies in it than a horror film. It's similar to the game. The game is not a horror game, not like *Resident Evil* where it's all about being in a scary situation – the game is all about having fun running through a crazy horde with silly characters. In that case, I think the *Dead Rising* adaptation is the perfect example of how to take a property and take it into something. I was a fan of the game, the people who were producing and writing it were from the game and love it. Capcom were in Vancouver, were involved. Because it was an online release we could give it straight to the audience to enjoy it rather than water it down. What I think the game is, I felt, is represented in the film. IGN accused it of being too faithful to the source material – which is hilarious because most movies get teased for not being faithful enough. But fans seem to like it. Each thing I do I try to get closer to what I want to do.

Some video games get a huge budget—what made Capcom want to do an online release?

I learned that the video game industry has no interest in doing adaptations. It was explained to me by producers of both video games and films: the video game industry is 10 times the size of the film industry. Films make 10 billion. Games make 100 billion. So they don't need the money. Not only that, but most video game adaptations have been terrible films and in the film industry they're used to taking a property and having their way with it and not involving the original creators.

From the video game perspective, handing over a property that is making them money and full creative control to a studio with no control, and not make no money and probably risk losing their franchise, there's no incentive to do that. That's why the *Halo* movie and all other movies didn't get made. In this case, Tim Carter is really in the world and knew the creators of the game and they knew he would do it right and would be included. With a small team, it would be more controlled and have a wide release. Legendary just created a digital division which was good for their brand, all the people involved were doing it for the right reasons. And being aware of what made that franchise great and bringing it to life rather than taking its name and turning it into something it isn't, like *Leprechaun*, so both sides of the coin there.

INTERVIEW WITH UWE BOLL

"Yeah, that was basically, maybe a bad idea"

Selected Filmography:

Postal
In The Name Of The King
In The Name Of The Kind 2: Two Worlds
In The Name Of The Kind 3: The Last Mission
Seed
Far Cry
Bloodrayne
Bloodrayne 2: Deliverance
Bloodrayne 3: The Third Reich
Blubberella
Rampage
Rampage: Capital Punishment
Rampage: President Down

You had a PhD before going into filmmaking, is that correct?

That was parallel. I did the *German Fried Movie* during when I was at university and then I kept studying. I was interested in this kind of film analytics and stuff. My masters exam was about the TV show Dallas. I felt there's not a lot of stuff actually written about TV series, TV shows, where they're coming from, what are the influences and how they function. And so I went into a master work on TV.

What was the transition into filmmaking from higher education?

I mean, I always wanted to make movies, that's the thing. For me, it was basically the other way around, I kept studying in the case that I have to turn into a teacher or if I turn into a journalist in the end, because I was not like sure that it will fly. That I actually will have a chance to make movies. So it was basically a kind of trying to be secure later, to have a job. That is the reason I stayed so long at university.

You were studying in Germany?

Yes, in Cologne and Cologne is the biggest university in Germany, actually. And that is like close to my hometown too, so I could basically stay at my parents' place and didn't have to pay any rent somewhere.

Once you started making films, I was kind of wondering how you knew which films you'd make sequels to and develop into franchises?

You know, that came later. When I did *House of the Dead* basically, and that it turned out to be the biggest financial success I had even if it was the worst reviews I ever got. And then with going out there and trying to get more video game based movies, so that was for me a reason to keep doing it.

How mindful are you of the potential of certain films you are making developing into franchises?

Yes. I mean, that was basically the era of video game based movies I did and at this point, age or whatnot, so many video game based movies done. At that point, they were just starting. Before, in the earlier years there wasn't, cause of street fights or wing commander. And I was basically riding on that wave. I made a lot of them and acquired various video games; *Dungeon Siege*, *BloodRayne*, *Far Cry*. For a lot of those movies it made sense to do a second part. *BloodRayne* has three parts, *In the Name of the King* has three parts, *Alone in the Dark* has two, *House of the Dead* has two. Only for *Postal* and *Far Cry*, I never did a second part.

I read online, you were enthusiastic to make another *Postal*

My favorite video game based movie that I did was *Postal* and it's too bad that the financial success of *Postal* was really bad even though there was a big following and a lot of like, fans. But it didn't really pay out financially. So I could never make a part two.

Was there a plan in making more entries in your established franchises like *BloodRayne* or *In The Name of the King?*

No, I wanted to do *BloodRayne* 4 in contemporary time and I was scheduled to do the movie two or three years ago but Majesco, the video game company, is not allowing any more movies. The third part of *In the Name of the King* didn't did so good. It was mostly 20 Century Fox helping me make the movies, and they said we really don't want a part four. So that was for me, the moment where it was also like, I stopped and thought, okay, *In the Name of the King* is also dead.

I'm basically finished with video game based movies. It costs millions to license the rights. And the time when it started with *House of the Dead* or *Alone in the Dark*, it was like $150,000 or $200,000 to buy the rights. So it was more affordable to do it.

So when you were making BloodRayne 3, what was the idea to do *Blubberella* alongside it?

Yeah, that was basically, maybe a bad idea. I liked working with Lindsey Hollister on Postal, she's hilarious, she's funny and I felt like why not use the whole setup of *BloodRayne* and make a funny *BloodRayne*, with a fat BloodRayne, and Lindsey was interested to do it. I said, "We won't have a lot of shooting time to do it. It's basically whatever we shoot five times the scene for *BloodRayne*, then you come in and we make one or two takes maximum, a joke scene apart."

The *BloodRayne* movies were always my worst experiences shooting. They were all very, very problematic to shoot. In Romania, in *BloodRayne* 1, the wild west city in *BloodRayne* 2, and the big accident where half of that city burnt down—biggest insurance case of all my movies. We couldn't shoot for two days. And then *BloodRayne* 3 in Croatia, it was winter, it was cold and the lead actress, Natassia Malthe, was problematic there. And nothing really worked, it was horrific with the crew as well. So I didn't really have enough time to give to Lindsey Hollister to do her shots, to do the *Blubberella* shots. So it added additional stress into the movie production and we were already running out of time. And it was really, in retrospect, a bad idea, but the movie is done. I think it's maybe thirty minutes, funny and another fifty minutes, shit. But if you say we do it, then we did it, right? But it was a mistake.

It's pretty interesting how you look back on your own career.

You know, you have to also admit mistakes and say, "Okay, that was a bad idea." But we did it in a way in *House of the Dead*, there's a *House of the Dead* funny version, but that was a different thing. Because we didn't have an extra for the funny version *of House of the Dead.* We basically used the same actors on set and played another scene because there's so many outtakes and stuff just doesn't work. I felt like *House of the Dead*, it didn't feel as funny as the outtakes and stuff. Let's make some scenes—we shoot them on purpose in an absurd way, like on purpose, it's funny. And all the actors had a lot of fun doing it, they were almost waiting for the take that they could shoot in an absurd way after the other shots were done. That was different. With *Blubberella*, to have a separate actress who was not involved in the *Blood-Rayne* series, it added additional pressure and everything. It was really problematic.

And obviously you've done more sequels with video games and *Rampage*. The box office success for *In the Name of the King* wasn't a huge hit. So what made the people greenlight two sequels?

No, just the production budget is also the sequels, it was more like we were low on trust fund. So I mean, the budget of the first one was $60 million, the budget of the sequels was $4 million. So the movie, *In the Name of the King 1*, did very well on DVD and TV. The worldwide gross on DVD only was around thirty million dollars. And then of course, if you say I make a second part just for DVD and TV, the buyers were excited about it. And so we could make some money there. Similar to *BloodRayne*, what was also theatrically a flop but it did very strong on DVD. So that a cheaper part two and part three made sense and *House of the Dead* and *Alone in the*

Dark, exactly the same. So it was basically a really monetary decision to say, "Let's do more parts of it but way cheaper", and then it worked in the DVD and TV market.

When you do these, do you worry about contradicting or repeating yourself? Or is that something you're not too worried about?

Yes. And I always wondered too, if I do a second part and so I am not interested to just do the same movie again, basically. So that was the reason why I went in *BloodRayne* always almost like a hundred years forward. So to have *BloodRayne 1* as a classical vampire movie, set in the 1700s somewhere and then going into the 1800, 1900 western, having a vampire western basically in *BloodRayne* 2. And then having a Second World War *BloodRayne* 3, I think makes sense and it's different. So you basically have totally different genres. That was the reason I was interested to do *BloodRayne* 4 playing in today's time.

If the second one was the western, what kind of genre would you say the fourth one would have been?

The fourth one would be more what we know from movies like—*Underworld* or *Blade* or stuff where it is a little more kind of science fiction? So I was really intrigued to do this. And *In the Name of the King* was—basically, we went from present day into medieval dragon time with part two and part three, went away from the big, big cult story of *King 1* to what was more like a *Lord of the Rings* compact kind of movie.

And *Alone in the Dark* 2 is actually based on the video game or that's how it came out. There was a mess up in *Alone in the Dark* because when I did my movie, Atari Infogrames was actually doing an *Alone in the Dark* video game. And then when my movie was finished, they didn't do the game. And then two or three years later, a new *Alone in the Dark* video game came out and then we found, "Okay, but now we follow the game in Central Park in New York and blah, blah, blah." So *Alone in the Dark* 2 follows actually *Alone in the Dark* 5 the video game better. My movie *Alone in the Dark* doesn't follows any specific game because they never finished that game as they were supposed to do.

Can you elaborate more on the kind of grief that sometimes comes along with working in franchises?

Yeah, in non-communication. You read things in the press sometimes without anybody ever contacting you. Game companies failed in putting a marketing concept together with the movie distribution company. Working together it pays on all levels. We saw that a film company in Montreal is doing their own CGI. And I tried contacting one of the biggest franchises they have and they don't even say they want to do the CGI for the movie. So there were too many differences to do anything on the movie. What is their game?

Did you ever want to make sequels you weren't able to?

Yeah, of course. Definitely. In the last eight, nine years, so many crazy things on the planet have happened. And so much stuff that is in *Postal* basically was visionary. We made jokes at this point where a lot of people were way too politically correct so that was interesting. Ten years later it all came true. It would be great to do *Postal 2*.

When the sequels to *House of the Dead* and *Alone in the Dark* were made, was it difficult to find another director taking over the reins for it?

Yes, on *House of the Dead*, I just sold the license to somebody else back to Mindfire Entertainment and they did part two with Lionsgate. I produced and shot *Alone in the Dark 2* in LA to get maximum amount of known actors as cheap as possible. And then I gave the director's job to Michael Roesch and Peter Scheerer because I've known them forever. I was only one time on set and had conferences with them. But I don't like it if producers are pushy.

And was it the same with *Seed*, because they have a sequel to that?

They came to me and said, "We really love your movie, *Seed*. We want to do a part two." The rest is completely different and I agreed to it under the circumstances that I could sell the movie so that it makes some commissions. I sold it to the same buyers as *Seed 1*. And of course they were very disappointed in the budget because the movie didn't turn out really good. And that was it with *Seed*, to be honest.

I guess it's kind of easier to continue horror franchises more than anything else.

Yeah and then you need all the parts of movies, of course—like a really good reason to make another part. Of course, comic book movies, video game based movies are like almost made for franchise, made for getting second part and third part.

Sounds like the directors must be pretty happy

to work with you. You must have been a pretty good boss.

Yeah, I think so. Right now we have *King Cobra* with James Franco, Christian Slater, Alicia Silverstone, Molly Ringwald. It's in post-production and they shot the movie, I had nothing to do with the story or whatever. But I made the movie happen in making it with a minimum guarantee.

So they got investments together to make the movie and then I have no problem with that. I strongly believe that the director should be the filmmaker, should be the creator of the movie and if somebody else wrote it and somebody else is the director, I probably have no, let's say, need or urge to be on that set. It's like I feel like, "No, let them do what they're supposed to do and let them make that movie."

Did you always envision *Rampage* as having more than one entry into it?

No, I wrote *Rampage* based on the kind of movie I really want to watch like, a movie with twists and turns, where you don't really know how this ends, who's good, who's bad. So I wrote *Rampage* like this, like a very ruthless script with ruthless character. The reviews were decent. So I felt after few years talking to Brendan Fletcher, okay, so see about *Rampage*. In the end, he had some money, he's running away. What then? Like what would happen to that.

And that is reason I followed it up and *Rampage* 2 that he wasn't hiding, he had some money. Well, he has in a way, wants to do more and got more politically involved. And that is basically why *Rampage* 2 happened. But when we pitched

Rampage 2, the market changed so drastically in a negative way, because of piracy and the shrinking of the DVD market. *Rampage* was always very harsh, it's not really good as a TV sale.

So the success of *Rampage* 2 was really low, was not even one-third of the revenue of *Rampage*. The only reason I want to do *Rampage* 3 is because I want to finish the story about the village It felt like my boyhood movie. You know, it's like we follow a mass murderer for nine years. And Brendan said, "Oh no, I don't believe this character got older." But it feels like it's an unfinished story. I want to finish it and I already know that I will make no money on that movie. I will maybe lose money, but it's also, right now it definitely looks like this will be the last movie I do.

So the market shifted to TV and series and *Avengers* movies, basically and the classical independent movie is dead. And too much money gets lost and there's too much money needed to keep staying in the film business that I will focus more on making other people's movies possible so my production company can still exist. We will still invest in other people's movies. But I don't see myself making any more movies because I've made too many movies. I'm not a film student anymore so I cannot like force myself to go cheaper and cheaper and cheaper and faster and faster and faster.

So right now if you start as a filmmaker, you're better making good movies for hundred thousand, two hundred thousand dollars production budget. And because if you spend more, you will lose money. And I mean that doesn't really, for that amount of money, I cannot work.

I mean, I suppose it's nice to kind of go around a project you're especially passionate about.

I mean, of course you always think, "Oh my god, I love being on set. I love making movies." I have a few scripts I would do, whatever. It only makes sense if you spend some money on it and right now the market doesn't give you that money back and based on this—I'm fifty now, that is in comparison to other directors that are young. But I would say I definitely will have a break for years to come. And based on the fact that selling other people's movies, I will always know exactly where the market is and I can come back in a few years if it makes sense.

Now you need Nicholas Cage in an action movie to recoup two million dollars, but Nicholas Cage wants two million to make the movie. So I mean you can shoot the movie, you can give him two million and you shoot the movie for three million in Bulgaria. You work your ass off and then in the end, you lose five hundred thousand dollars. It doesn't make any sense. So the actor fees and the production costs are still high in comparison to what the market pays you back. And we could make a blockbuster on the early movies like *House of the Dead* or *Alone in the Dark*, they made like twenty, thirty million DVD gross worldwide. A movie like *House of the Dead* would now make a million DVD gross. Total.

Japan paid for *BloodRayne* and *Alone in the Dark*, a million bucks per movie. They pay me now for *Rampage*, ten thousand dollars. That is what happened to the movie. So the bit torrents of the world together with super cheap YouTube, Hulu, Netflix, only paying for some preview product enormous amounts of money, but for the majority of the product they buy, they pay almost nothing. They destroyed it single-handed, it's over.

You haven't licensed your films onto Netflix?

No, they are on Netflix, of course it's licensed to everybody who's there. But the money you get, it's like a joke in comparison to what you could get from a blockbuster before, all DVD rental income, the DVD sales rank was high. It was really high ten years ago, eight years ago and then it dropped down faster than you could blink. That is a big problem.

You'll be out to survive in the film industry financially?

Yeah, I mean, I made a lot of movies and I was lucky that I was able to make a lot of movies during a good time, especially DVD revenues and TV paid even better. And so I have enough money for myself as long as I don't like, buy a Ferrari. But just keep my money together. I'm good. And that is a good thing. But overall, the last three, four years was a real struggle and you hope really like the market has to recover, it has to get better. Companies must pay a little more money to make it worthwhile for you to keep making movies.

Do you get a lot of interest?

There are a lot of people that make one movie but they don't make another movie. A lot of high up people in the world they always want you to find an investor or whatever, somebody from your group of friends that can put the money together. Now you make you hundred-thousand-dollar movie and get good reviews. And people talk about you and they want to do another movie for maybe three hundred thousand, four hundred thousand and then you hit the brick wall because you're not getting investors, you're not getting anything, you're not getting the sales. Then you're forced to do another hundred- thousand-dollar movie and then you're basically done. And that is what happens to a lot of young filmmakers right now.

Every week I get a movie offer or somebody who just shot it and is trying to sell it. And there's nobody in them, no name actor, movie star that makes between okay and shit and they don't sell anymore. Like ten, fifteen years ago, you could video release a movie on DVD with a good cover even if it had no name actors, if you created a good cover. You sold the DVD. Now, you do a good cover with a shitty movie and they don't sell it anymore. You can basically sell only on Amazon, and who's going to buy it, because nobody knows about it.

I guess, it's probably not worth asking you how to get involved in movies as a writer then.

No I mean, it's like—basically I'm not a good writer in a way that I consider I write something. I can write only stuff where I feel I have something to say. These kinds of movies are personally emotional for me but it takes forever. Like *Rampage* 3 is still not completely finished and I've been working on it for a year and I'm updating it and changing it constantly. So I'm really not a writer for hire at all. That would never work and I was never able to write anything whether it was *In the Name of the King* or *BloodRayne* or whatever, I could never do it. And of course, a lot of writers are contacting me and saying, "I'll write script, you want to make a movie or produce the movie." But it's so bad, the market, that I really have to tell them like, "Sorry, it's a waste of time. I am not getting a script into production. The money is not there." Like nothing will happen. So what movies you can shoot is let's say, Jason Statham is doing it for free or he's doing it in a way like whatever, saying, "I get 25% of the revenues instead of my 5 million dollars I want as an actor." And then maybe you can make a movie with Jason Statham.

$5 million, huh?

Yeah, he wants $5 million. It's a lot of money. This is what I mean. It's like Jason Statham, Bruce Willis, John Travolta. How many movies you saw from these guys in the last few years, they were not even in the movie theaters anymore. They were only on Netflix, they were only on cable, they were only on DVD. So how they can justify to get paid millions, they're not worth it. There are only like, four or five people left who are always going theatrical and although, these guys had flops like Leonardo DiCaprio, Will Smith, Tom Cruise, you know. But they are only working theatrical if they do the right movies.

How do you feel looking back at your filmography?

I feel my filmography is a lot, producer or director, you know. A lot of movies up on it where I, as a filmmaker and director and writer whatever, was not really involved. But I just executed the movie as a director, as a producer, telling myself that is good business, we have to do it. And from the, I don't know, 32, 33 movies I did, I feel good about around 12 of them. They don't really matter and I wrote them and I'm very proud of them. You know, movies about the Vietnam War, Auschwitz, Wall Street, *Rampage 1 and* 2, *Postal* and are movies that I'm really proud of.

Being invested in art is the key theme that I'm seeing coming up in these conversations.

I mean, look at the other video game based directors, they make only popcorn movies, they—I don't see them as filmmakers in a way what I am. They are directors and they make things that are fun to do, and they make a lot of money with it. And they are produced by the studios and they are all about franchises. And a lot of others are very producer-driven like *Indiana Jones*. Even if Steven Spielberg would not shoot the new *Indiana Jones*, it still is a George Lucas franchise, you know.

And in a lot of the franchises of the Marvel comic book heroes, I think it's very, very producer-driven and the directors are basically tools that are like—they always say, "Oh, the director brought so much into it," but basically, they have a script, that have a pre-visual storyboard, mood boards and the director has to fucking follow them or he gets fired. I mean, if you do *Fantastic Four* or whatever movie like this, you follow what they tell you because they're pre-testing the script and do all kinds of things to finally shoot the movie and surprisingly not, that movie will still suck big time. So that's interesting.

What films have you been digging recently?

I have watched most of the stuff on DVD now and I saw movies on DVD where you think like, "Why the fuck did that movie ever get made?" Yes, I've watched Adam Sandler in *The Cobbler* and now I know why I ever watched it, so it was like, dead on arrival, and a lot of the movies with A-list stars are getting made and they're getting instantly buried. I watched a movie with Ben Stiller where he was a camera guy doing a documentary and that movie was also, really bad.

So that is a lot of money still in the business. What gets spent and lost from investors and I think the reason for it is what I have pointed out about *Rampage 2* — the rich getting richer. You have basically, a few thousand people that have so much money that they really don't care. You know like Larry Ellison from Oracle, whose daughter is just doing—making one shitty movie after the other. But she doesn't care if she loses two hundred million, pappy has forty-five billion. So and I mean that is the thing where there are a lot of people who have really deep pockets and they are bored. And then they think, "Oh, what the fuck, let's make a few movies." Jim Shore from eBay with Participant Media is shooting a lot of movies and losing a lot of money. But this money makes it hard for people like me to get the actors cheaper, for example. Because they're still getting booked from people with money and that is the reason they're still getting away with charging millions in acting fees even for movies that are not even making the screen anymore.

I watch a lot of TV stuff, what I really like is leftovers from HBO, excellent TV series that air for short time, excellent TV series. *The Good Wife,* excellent. Of course, *House of Cards, Narcos,* on Netflix. Shows like *Breaking Bad* are just better written than any movie being produced right now.

DEVELOPMENT

There is a line between homage, parody and fan fiction, in the same way that there is a notable difference between remakes and reboots. When creators first create, usually inspired by a piece of work that makes them realise that they can do the exact same thing, their influence shows. At school, when I had finished reading *Fight Club* and was on an early Palahniuk binge, I wrote a story for a class that was so awful and heavily inspired that if I found a copy of it now, I'd burn it. It was a story called 'Enterprise of The Hurt' about a student who viewed relationships in a similar way as business transactions, seducing and being cruel. That was no doubt inspired by my impending desire to lose my virginity, as well over a dozen viewings of *Cruel Intentions*. The story was well received by my teacher but the fact that I didn't research enough or cite sources meant I didn't get a good grade, and ultimately foreshadowed my whole academic career.

Looking back, I realise that it was my first foray into writing and it never would have been that good, and whenever I hear stories of people who produce home runs on their first try I'm always skeptical. It was undoubtedly a rip off and now the style of it is far from how I would write it, and in a way I am still writing it as a novel, less misogynistic and more of an analysis of misogyny. I think one of the reasons that I'm writing it is the power to rewrite history. I can take something that makes me uncomfortable and alter it into something I'm proud of, this rip-off will become its own standalone piece of art, and it'll be rewritten into a positive experience.

Of course, art is full of these kinds of experiences. 50 *Shades* started as *Twilight* fan fiction, the *Alien Versus Predator* franchise was quickly ushered along by the Xenomorph head appearing in the background as a trophy in *Predator* 2, something that was a homage but quickly helped collide two major franchises. It seems the only major thing that bothers people about the difference between all of these influences is if the end result is good. Goodreads is a fantastic place to observe this. Reviews for first novels by indie authors tend to either lean towards praise for being fresh, or criticisms that they're just a rip off of other authors. This isn't necessarily an unfair criticism. There was a lecturer at university who spent over an hour defending his own novel from criticisms and reviews. Despite how much I'm talking about myself and my journey, I don't want to reach that level of self-indulgence.

With horror films, there appears to be much more of a fine line. People want their slasher to be the same, yet grow tired of seeing the same movie over and over, causing a bit of a paradox for the directors and writers. If we've already seen five films of the same character getting gruesome kills, is it unfair for a filmmaker to try and put a spin on it? To me, it doesn't seem unfair that Jason loses his mask briefly, or that Freddy tries to tell some jokes, because by this point the franchise has become familiar and safe, and that's the complete opposite objective of horror. That's why over the past few years films like *Hereditary, It Follows, Don't Breathe, Get Out* and *A Quiet Place* have conquered popular culture because they make us feel uncomfortable in the familiar world.

When I was younger, I used to have vivid nightmares. I would have this reoccurring character come for me, like a cross between the characters from *Spy vs. Spy* and a medieval doctor. It had this large beak or mask that it would chase me with and peck me to death with the same pattern that a pigeon does to a discarded piece of bread. In one dream I was in a city and it was snowing. The killer knew where I was because it could see my footsteps in the snow and I was trying to reach my father who would fly me away on a motorcycle, but I would keep falling off or getting lost and then the creature would look for me. He was called Denny the Dingo for no reason other than I had no clue what a dingo was. I remember he made comments on other dreams, like he was aware that he was haunting me each time individually and making me wake up screaming each time. Looking back on it it's quite a sophisticated terror for someone who was around ten years old. I clearly watched too many horror movies as a kid, which now I see as a good thing.

As a result of these dreams and films, I've always been uncomfortable with the idea of someone breaking in to a safe place, the idea that someone is real and chasing me is much more frightening than fictional monsters. I never got scared at the *Alien* films but *The Strangers* was my worst nightmare. Perhaps that's why I don't write horror at all, I'm just trying to make sense of the real world I live in.

The same way that my dreams and fears inspired me when I

was young must feel like a holy rite of passage to these directors who get to help create another chapter to the story that frightened them growing up. Of course, the film might be seen as derivative, because it incorporates these characters, sometimes not adding much to them other than a body count, but it's still the artistic dream coming full circle with these directors having a chance to scare a new generation into falling in love with the terror of a legendary monster.

Directors are constantly trying to get their own original ideas in development, some that pay homage to the films that influenced them as a child, but they are their own pure creation. After making *Evil Dead* in 2013, Fede Àlvarez made *Don't Breathe*, which shows that they are not just influenced but influencers. *Don't Breathe* is a tense film that plays on sound, vision and the hunter / hunted dynamic. Throughout these interviews, one of the themes is that the directors take the jobs for love of the franchise, rather than just because they need a job to pay the bills. This may be a factor in their decision, as it would for anyone who gets a job offer. They want to make an entry for the fans because they are a fan, and as a creator and a fan, that is a kind of sincerity you don't get as much in other forms of entertainment.

Perhaps I'm biased, but these are artists who had the option to do something that most of us never got. In literature more than anything, unless you write *James Bond* young adult novels, it's unlikely that you'll get close to touching an existing franchise, so the homage you pay is in what you create, hopefully not too close, otherwise you'll be chastised for it. These directors are just paying back the influence that they received all those years ago. It would be naïve of them to walk into the project thinking that they're going to make the greatest film or all time, or perhaps even something that beats the original, but to have something that expands on what gives us nightmares, the reason why we shine a light in our closet and are afraid to have our feet dangling off our bed. They helped expand it, they chose to pay back, and for that we should be grateful. I think if I had the opportunity to contribute to a new *Halloween* film, or even a *Star Wars* entry, I would. Wouldn't you?

INTERVIEW WITH KEVIN YAGHER

"I wasn't supported enough and had to deal with things that most directors don't normally have to"

Selected Filmography:

Hellraiser: Bloodline
Sleepy Hollow
Tales From The Crypt

Where did your passion for films come from?

My father would take me and my older brother, Jeff, to see monster movies - like the original *Planet of the Apes* and *The 7th Voyage of Sinbad*, among others. I developed a fascination with those types of films. My brother was a big part of that process because we would talk about the films afterwards, which added a lot to each experience. Later on, I began to watch other classic films like *Casablanca* and *To Kill a Mockingbird*. Then I went through a Hitchcock phase, which I still haven't come out of. But it was those very early days that set me in the direction of loving film.

You've worked on franchises like *Children of the Corn, Nightmare on Elm Street* and *Hellraiser*. How does it feel to have been involved in some of the most influential franchises in horror, and why do you think fans are so loyal to these films?

I was thinking to myself a few months back, getting ready for the Texas Frightmare convention, that I've done Jason's makeup in *Friday the 13th* 4, Freddy's in *A Nightmare on Elm Street* 2,3 &4, made Chucky in *Child's Play* 1,2,3 & 4, The Crypt Keeper from HBO's *Tales from the Crypt* and then also got to direct Pinhead in *Hellraiser: Bloodline*. And I might as well throw in – writing the screenplay for *Sleepy Hollow* (Directed by Tim Burton, starring Johnny Depp). Anyway, I thought WOW, that's a lot of horror icons. Don't know anyone else that's done that. It's been very cool to have been lucky enough to do that. I'm very proud of that and feel blessed.

To answer the second question, I think that horror fans are so loyal to horror because they love to be frightened or scared without actually experiencing any real danger. They love the adrenaline and thrill that they go through, the experience it brings (like a skydiver does when jumping out of a plane). And they feel they can watch those films over and over without getting bored. And soon the film's characters become a part of them.

What led you into directing, was that always the goal?

I didn't set out to be a director. I just wanted to break into the film business and go to work for somebody like Dick

Smith or Rick Baker. After I started my own company, I began to think about directing. It wasn't until I started working on *Tales from the Crypt* that I knew I wanted to direct. Building the Crypt Keeper was a fantastic job. I got to design and sculpt him then bring him to life animatronically and finally, after Bob Zemeckis stepped aside, I was able to direct all the Crypt Keeper's wrap- arounds and later two of the show's episodes. During those experiences, I fell in love with directing.

When you started directing *Hellraiser: Bloodline*, were you familiar with the franchise or did you have to go back to explore the lore?

I was familiar with *Hellraiser*, but I did go back and watch the first three films over and over to really absorb myself into that world, the world of Clive Barker. At first I didn't think that I could bring anything new to the franchise, until I read Pete Atkins' script, which was really well done. I loved the fact that it explored the history and creation of the box, the doorway into hell. I also really liked that the story took place in three different time periods, which I thought would be challenging and very exciting.

How do you feel looking back at the film now, especially after taking an Alan Smithee credit?

It's funny, I happen to be online looking something up and I ran across a few minutes of *Bloodline* and sat and tried to watch it with my wife. I was explaining to her which scenes were mine and which shots came after I left, etc. Before I knew it, I started remembering what had taken place and how the whole thing had sort of disintegrated during and after shooting including my relationship with Dimension Films. Before I knew it, I was getting angry and then depressed, ha! I think it's difficult for anyone who works so hard on something to have it not turn out the way they had hoped. I felt that I wasn't protected by producers from the studio and I wasn't supported enough and had to deal with things that most directors don't normally have to. The whole experience was somewhat painful but eventually I will sit down and watch the film again. I really want to do that. I think it will be therapeutic.

Over the years you've done effects and work on so many iconic films, how have the changes in Hollywood filmmaking affected your work?

When CGI came into existence, it didn't have a whole lot of effect on my work. At that time, it was just an enhancement upon what I and other make up effects artists were doing. But within the years to follow it became evident that our work was going to slow and suffer because of it. It pretty much took away animatronic puppet work and creature suit work from us. Many of my workers went off to start learning digital design and Zbrush in order to continue creating creatures even if they were to be digital. There is still a lot of make-up prosthetic work left to do, but the jobs are fewer and far between. Some shops have supplemented work by doing more commercials rather than film and television and also working on practical effects jobs in amusement parks. Some have even started building model kits, collectibles and going back to their original love of mask making. I am extremely happy that I was able to work in the effects field from the beginning, through the peak and even into this slowed down period.

What was it like working with Clive Barker, was his vision of the film different to the final result?

Clive was a fantastic person to me. He was supportive at the very beginning, but unfortunately wasn't around too much after that because he went off to prep and shoot his movie *Lord of Illusions*. I don't have a whole lot to say about his vision of *Bloodline* prior to the shooting of it. Most of my creative meetings were with the writer Peter Atkins.

What have you been working on recently?

I finished a 12 year run, doing the effects work for the TV series *Bones* and I've been working on other TV projects and some independent films as well. I'm also in talks about doing another exciting film project which, unfortunately, I can't talk about just yet.

With *Hellraiser*, if you'd known how the production would have been would you have accepted the job?

I have thought about that exact question quite often over the years and I have to answer honestly, which is no I wouldn't have. At the time, I had several other offers for films that were less known or original concepts. Looking back, I definitely would've taken one of them instead.

The *Hellraiser* franchise has had a turbulent continuation recently, does this cause any reaction in you?

Not really. When I left *Bloodline* behind I really don't think about that franchise at all. Nor do I think about the company that owns it. However, I must say that it's pretty ironic given what has happened to half of that company presently, with the #ME TOO movement and all. Perhaps karma does exist. Regardless I think it's time for Dimension Films to pass on the *Hellraiser* franchise to someone else who can resurrect it and bring it into a new light or shall I say, *into a new DARKNESS.*

INTERVIEW WITH MARY LAMBERT

"They want to stay involved in the fantasy world."

Selected Filmography:

Pet Sematary
Pet Sematary Two
Halloweentown II: Kalabar's Revenge
Urban Legends: Bloody Mary

What is it about sequels that captures the imagination of audiences?

I think that a lot of the current trends in television and cable series have grown out of the success of franchise films. When an audience becomes interested or even obsessed with a character or group of characters they want MORE stories about the character. They want to stay involved in the fantasy world. This sort of episodic storytelling actually works best in the television format as evidenced by popular shows that run for many seasons. But when a movie really keys into the zeitgeist of the time it can also endure many iterations or sequels.

INTERVIEW WITH PETER WEBBER

"Well, the film came out. I think it made close to $100 million, and got to #2 in the American box office chart and it got that heat of really bad reviews, so I got used to being pummeled by critics."

Selected Filmography:

Girl With A Pearl Earring
Hannibal Rising
Emperor
Earth: One Amazing Day

So, did you get to spend much time with Thomas Harris, creator of the *Hannibal* character?

I spent a lot of time with Thomas Harris. You're going to hate this because one evening we had finished working and went out. He's got a very nice place right on the shoreline of Miami. I asked him who Hannibal Lecter was based on, and he told me this story in detail, and I've forgotten most of the story because we were drinking that evening. That's terrible, but perhaps it's for the best. I really enjoyed working with him. I don't think he's a fan of the movie, to be honest and I haven't spoken to him since then. One of the things that has recently changed is that the mythos has expanded because of *Hannibal* the TV show. Which I still haven't watched.

It's good.

Yeah, everyone tells me this. And if they'd gone to another season, Martha, one of the producers, had written me an email and I would have directed an episode, but it was cancelled.

It would have been really cool for that to come full circle

Ha-ha, well I'm sure I would have gotten a lot of hate. I'll give you one example of some of the hate mail I get. A week ago, I got a tweet from a Spanish person something like "Thank you very much because of your shitty film I've lost two hours of my life" with a little GIF of Leonardo DiCaprio pointing his finger. And then I couldn't reply, sadly, because he blocked me.

How do you feel when that comes through?

I don't reply. Listen, it was a long time ago, there have been some horrible TV reviews. When you've been doing this as long as I have you win some you lose some. I had much more fun making the film than some people had watching it.

Do you think Thomas Harris will ever write or publish anything ever again?

I don't know, he doesn't need to. Especially, I'd think, with more book sales that accrue through TV series, he's being paid for the rights bla bla bla... I think he's got a nice little pension. He takes a while to write a book. I know he was working on something else that sounded very interesting–a period thing about this group of thieves. Who knows, maybe he's writing about that or maybe he's stopped. I don't really keep in touch with him.

I heard that he was pressured into writing *Hannibal Rising*

Well when you say pressured, that sounds like there were thugs at the door leaning over his shoulder. It was his own decision and no one forced him to do anything. Dino De Laurentiis told him that people want to learn about the origins of Hannibal Lecter in a film. Thomas decided, after a little persuasion maybe, that he would do that. He was paid very handsomely and said that he wanted to write the script and there we go. I'm sure his publisher must have said to him that you should have a book as well as this being a script. I'm not sure about there being pressure, commercial pressure maybe. If you look at the early iterations of the novels and the style of writing, they're changed.

With *Hannibal Rising*, it's the novel that Martin Amis said, slightly homophobically, that Thomas Harris had turned gay. The earlier books are purer. I don't know how it worked with him, writing the book and writing the script and in what order they were done. So, no, I wouldn't say that he was forced, but perhaps he didn't do it for the right reasons. He may have been disappointed afterwards!

Was there a disappointment that you couldn't get Antony Hopkins back?

Dino wanted him to do a cameo, and wanted to it to be like bookends. It was a terrible idea and I'm not sure how it would have worked. Anthony Hopkins sat there in an armchair saying, "let me tell you about my childhood..."

Let me tell you about two Easter eggs that I hid in there that people didn't really seem to pick up on. Maybe that's because the people who enjoyed the film haven't seen many films. There's a guy who stabs someone through the head, that's modeled on Sergio Leone, the shots as the two are looking at each other before the knife is plunged into him. The biggest homage in the film is to Melville, the French director, the name at the village he goes into at the end to see the final killer is called Melville.

What made you go into filmmaking?

The thing that started me on the journey, and I didn't start that young, was when I was 15 or 16 I saw a Godard film, as a pretentious teenager I kept hanging around the cinema and that was that. It really sealed the idea for me that there was someone behind the camera, playing with the form really. It took until the mid-80s, when I applied to film school. It was different working on TV back then. It's wasn't just dancing shows and American imports, there were some really important documentaries being made back then.

What was the transition to going into feature films?

Luck – being in the right place at the right time. I worked with this company that made hour long documentaries and two of the guys who were working there were working on a film. I was working with them making another film that all fell apart and they lost their director on *Girl With A Pearl Earring* and it just happened that at university I did a degree in History of Art. Funnily enough the first film I ever did any work on may be getting made in the near future, so I'll actually get to make my debut film finally!

And the reception to *Girl With The Pearl Earring* was pretty outstanding.

Yeah it was. It was an amazing experience. One minute I

was shooting a BBC Drama in some backstreets and the next I was at the Chateau Marmont in Los Angeles.

Well if you speak to Scarlett Johansson feel free to pass her on my phone number.

Haha, I haven't spoken to Scarlett since the publicity for *Girl With The Pearl Earring*. She turned 18 on the set, she's such a major star now.

This is pre-*Lost In Translation*?

Lost In Translation hadn't come out. She flew from Tokyo from the set of *Lost In Translation* to Luxemburg where we were filming. She's fantastic.

After *Girl With The Pearl Earring* you must have gotten a lot more attention.

Yeah, of course. It didn't win many of them but we got shed loads of nominations. 11 Bafta nominations, 3 Oscar nominations, some Golden Globe nominations and we won a bunch of festivals in Europe, so doors open. And one of them that opened was the film with Dino. And partly I took it, it's not like I wasn't aware of the whole Hannibal Lecter thing, I'd seen all the films and read the books. It was as much to work with Dino–he's worked with David Lynch, Wachowskis, and there he was at 89 years old, pumped full of energy, it was as much that opportunity, really. It was sometimes really great to work with him and sometimes really frustrating. He was an old boy, he's been around.

One of the funny things about him, they don't shoot with sound in Italy, they post-sync everything because when American movies came in rather than being shown with subtitles they were played with Italian audio. So, the Italians have gotten used to the sound and lip movements may not be together. It doesn't work anywhere else! Sometimes he would just get the actors to speak numbers instead... so Dino had no concept of who should be quiet while shooting, so his phone would go off in the middle of takes or he would be shouting "pronto pronto!"

Was there lots of reading up on the lore to establish yourself with the franchise?

Tonally, what Tom had written, what I had to go from was the script he had written. What he created was unlike the other works. We tried to get some of the creepiness in there with the production design and I think we did a great job in the giant vat thing one of the guys drowned in.

What was the move after the release of the film?

Well, the film came out. I think it made close to $100 million, and got to #2 in the American box office chart and it got that heat of really bad reviews, so I got used to being pummeled by critics. I mean, fair enough, I'm used to it now but it was upsetting at the time. It was a long time ago now. One of the things that has changed my point of view is that I've discovered through Twitter and the like that there is a constituency, perhaps not a large one, there's a constituency that regard it as a cult film and really like it. The way people write about it like the look on Gaspard's face when he first gets blood on it, it's got some moments there that adolescence of a certain sensibility seem to like it. Also, young Americans seem to like it, there's like 3 or 4 strong constituencies for it, and the rest are the haters. After that it was difficult for me to get a job because the reviews were so bad and people expected it to make much more money.

I took a while and the next movie I made was *Emperor* in New Zealand, but there was quite a large gap between them. Another thing is that sometimes you can spend time trying to get your own films off the ground, there are scripts that come to you and there are scripts that you are trying to get made, and you can spend a couple of years on a project that you're passionate about that you raise the finance for or you find the actor and then you lose one element or the other and you're just about to go... I've spent a lot of time; too much time with these kinds of films. I think now I'll accept more jobs as they come up. You can drive yourself mad waiting waiting waiting, and the world has changed as well. Netflix allowing you to stream things has changed the game and made theatrical release less important. You've got a lot of money going into very few movies, mostly people dressed in lycra with special effects. The area that I've worked in is mainly drama and historical dramas, that's shrunk significantly because of TV. It's a good time for TV whether you like Norwegian crime drama or *Game of Thrones* or *House of Cards*, so the world is changing.

How do you feel about the films you've turned down?

It's like a fish tank. There are these big juicy pellets that drop down and the big fish are up at the top, people like Ridley Scott, by the time the pellets get down to me they're not so big and juicy. A lot of the scripts that get to me need a bunch of work. It can take a long time, and sometimes scripts don't get there, and you can spend a year or two developing, very rarely does some- thing come in that's just good enough. One of the reasons I did *Ten Billion* was a passion project. I did *Tutankhamun* for ITV which was pretty fun to shoot, and because it's TV it means the money is on the table. And I got to go to South Africa for 6 months so it could be worse!

SECOND INCITING INCIDENT

It's December and I have two weeks to finish this book and hand it into my editors. I've spent the last month neglecting it, as the deadline becomes more and more inevitable with every Christmas song that I have to hear. I don't think there's been a month or two where I've felt less like a writer than this one, and here I am, punching keys on an overpacked train and watching the word count go up and up and wondering if I'm making up for lost time or delaying the inevitable. I think Hollywood likes to show writers as successful and accomplished people because it makes the actual writer who wrote the damn thing feel like they're way better off than they are. Perhaps on career day a cup of black coffee and self-doubt isn't exactly the biggest enticement to being an artist.

In the years since I signed the contract for this book, my respect for these filmmakers has only grown because they've hustled much harder in their craft than I have in this new stage of my adulthood. The past year was a full one for me. I finished my Master's degree, moved to a new city, bought a flat, got a couple of jobs, made new friends and all of this made it that much harder and more exhausting to come home and try to create art. I think the truth of the matter is that no matter how much I want to try and create something that expresses how I feel it does drain something out of me. It takes the small amount of energy that I have left, and it's usually hard enough to go to work or try to be social and then commit to pouring myself out in the evening. Sometimes I feel like I'm driving on a route, and each objective that I need to have a healthy life means I have to pull over, to eat, stretch my legs, whatever — but the issue is that each time I do this it means that I won't make it there in time; by trying to have all these goals in my life concurrently I'm ultimately putting certain areas of my life towards disappointment, until something else is a bigger priority and the destination changes.

Shortly said, there are two ways to think about it:

1) I'm not actually a writer. Despite me typing that sentence, and every other one that precedes and succeeds existing as a rebuttal, it's possible. Writing could just be my most longest running hobby yet, in the same way I played guitar or took karate classes as a kid, only to quit a few weeks later. Philosophical and theological debates aside, it's possible that it's not what I'm meant to be doing on this planet and is a culmination of positive reinforcement, something that I happened to be clever and resourceful at and had (until recently) a strong work ethic.

2) My personality and life and commitment to art isn't necessarily defined by my bibliography and productivity. The fact that I'm 25 years old, at the time of writing, and focusing somewhat on my career, social life and trying to save financially, is normal, and that the fact that I don't bust out tweets about the craft or books every year doesn't define the love and time I've put into literature, particularly independent literature. Perhaps falling short of a Goodreads challenge doesn't mean I'm less committed than my Face-

book friends who reviews books and are better at time management than me. Perhaps part of growing up and being adult is finding this balance and I'm new in this area.

Of course, there could be a third option, in the same way that it's possible for a coin to land on its edge rather than heads or tails. Though, these are the two options that I think are the most likely. I'm not sure what the answer is; my heart tells me #2 is true while #1 exists just as an element of self doubt that's been festering in some artistic downtime. Because, ultimately - I'm not defined by the amount of books I read, review or write. Donna Tartt releases one almost every decade, some crime writers release several a year.

Perhaps if I spend less time worrying about my bibliography, and more time on the craft, then I'll have a healthier and much more achievable end goal. This is the most realistic option in retrospect, but often it feels like the simplest things to see are often the hardest, and when you're looking forward you're often blinded by the headlights rather than wondering what the other car's seeing as it drives past.

The reason I'm projecting my anxieties here is because I feel they are not solely my own. The same delays, worries, creative blocks and outcomes I've had are no doubt exclusive to me, you, or even the directors who have been kind enough to volunteer their insight for this book. Ultimately, it's decades of planning, meetings, unrealised projects and seeing what is available that lead to their filmography, and it's much more complicated behind the surface than just what can be seen from scrolling through their IMDB page. Perhaps I'm as guilty of making this judgement about them more than anyone else, because not only did I think it but I made myself wonder why. It's not a question that has such a definitive answer, nor is it a question that is going to stop being asked.

A *Halloween* sequel was released this year, and while not terrifying it felt like a worthwhile sequel, but it also dismissed all the other sequels that came before it, establishing a confusing timeline of alternate realities that ultimately makes me want to rename The Shape into The Mess. By the time this book is being held in your hand, there'll have been a fair few new superhero releases, some of which I'll have paid to go see in the cinema. The future is bright, financially motivated, scary and full of art. Like a Venn diagram that overlaps in so many different ways, sometimes it's difficult to figure out what's next and how to react to it. Do we take it in the big studio way and map out a plan that's eventually reinforced with financial returns, or do we take it indie style, one title at a time and see what's next?

For me, it's going back to what makes me happy. I'm going to read some more and declutter my brain, I'm going to have a beer in a bar when I've submitted this book, and then have many more when everyone is happy with it. I'm going to attack the projects that I want to write, the novel, short stories, everything under the sun that I feel that I can offer. Some of which will see the light of day and others will be buried deeper than any ritual can bring to life. I think the truth here is that as a creator I am scared, that sometimes it's not good enough, that I'm not good enough, and that if the one thing that I think I may have a halfway chance of doing well and contributing to on this spinning little rock is terrible — then what's left for me? My books are my children, each word, the DNA that I plan to leave behind after I'm gone, under the naive hope that one day someone will find something I've written and it could mean something to them too.

When I look back on myself in the future, I hope I have the same level of clarity, determination and honesty of the people in these books. Just like being in a successful band, it might be annoying to have to sing that famous song that everyone knows every set, when actually you just wanna play your new album, but surely you must also be happy that at least people are singing along? When I create, I feel calmer, like I'm floating, and the tension and bad thoughts that usually fill my mind momentarily alleviate. To some people, those that don't know me or don't know why I pursue this rabbit-hole of creativity, it may seem strange. Though perhaps it's that inner strangeness that I really value in myself, and others, the kind of strangeness that can give pleasure and importance to the simplest and most absurd moments in life. The strangeness where you can have that discussion and fascination with things and that makes it all the more special to you. If there are two paths in the woods, I'll want the one less travelled, even if it means I'm being chased by cannibal hillbillies. So if there's anyone else out there that has a brain filled with popular culture and random knowledge, this one's for you, stay weird out there.

INTERVIEW ERNIE BARBARASH

"I find doing sequels and prequels in a real way is very much like the theatre."

Selected Filmography:

Cube Zero
Stir of Echoes: The Homecoming
6 Bullets
Christmas In The Wild

I imagine for you, it might not be as interesting talking about some of your older films compared to the newer ones.

It's funny, I always joke saying that I have deeper fondness for a film once it's been a few years because when you're making it, you're just really aware of either the flaws, or the things you wish you would have done with it that you didn't have time to do. I started doing theatre before I did film, I find doing sequels and prequels is very much like the theatre.

So, the world has sort of been set up for you, and you can reimagine it, you can massage it, you can manipulate it, but you still have source material to work from. In a way, that's very interesting; it's a different kind of challenge, because you can just create whatever, so in a way before you can create your sequel and prequel, you have to go and really figure out; what's at the core of the first part of this that you weren't involved in that makes it work. The smart way to do it is, before you go, "Let me do my own thing," you have to figure out what the old thing was and what worked about it, and what you think that people would follow, the fans, the audience, the core audience really would love to see more of.

Sometimes you're successful, sometimes you're not, but it's that extra exploratory detective work that you wouldn't do on something that's completely original, or you're working with the original writer.

How did you get interested in films and start your career?

It's funny, I've talked about this very explicitly, I never intended to go into film, I was always a theatre guy, I wanted to direct theatre since I was like 14 years old, and I directed my first play when I was 15. I studied theatre and I went to university for theatre degrees and I worked in theatre in New York, in between college and graduate school.

Then, I was finishing my directing in New York at Club UN. I had a job lined up for right after I graduated, being the assistant director on a big Broadway musical, and it just so happened that just before we went into rehearsal they postponed that by about four or five months, the start of rehearsal. I knew that I needed a job, but I didn't have my green card at the time, I had a special Visa, so I couldn't just go work at Starbucks, I don't even think we had Starbucks back then, but I just couldn't go find a temp job doing something else; I had to find a job in my field and what I studied.

I found this little Canadian film company that had just opened a New York office that needed somebody to help out in the office, and that little film company turned out a few years later to be Lionsgate. What happened was that they gave me kind of a development, and said, "What would it take for you not to go back, what would it take for you to stay on full-time for us?" I said, "If you help me get a green card," because no theatre in the US was able to do that, because it takes a lot of time, money and effort to do that. And, they said, "Sure."

So, I ended up, that company, which was called at the time Cinepix, or Cinepix Film Properties, and that was a company that was run out of Montreal, where I had grown up, and it was run by John Dunning and Andre Link, who are the two Canadian producers who started people like Ivan Reitman. That was their company, and they were great mentors and they were great bosses to work for. I started by being a production executive for them and after a short while they would send me oversee to little movies in the Ukraine or in Montreal or all over the place. I started being a producer on the movies, and that was sort of my film school. Then, through them I ended up being a producer on some really interesting theatrical films like *American Psycho*, and a Peter Bogdanovich movie called, *The Cat's Meow*, among others. Then, I was producing for a while, then I felt like I really missed directing and doing more of the creative work myself.

One day we were sitting in the sound mix with Mike Paseornek for the sequel to *Cube*, called *HyperCube*, and I had an idea for a prequel, and I turned to Mike and to Peter Block, who at the time was also at Lionsgate. I said, "Hey guys, I have an idea for a prequel to this, let me pitch it to you. If you like it, will you let me write and direct it, because I want to get back into directing?" And they said, "Sure."

So, I was very lucky because of Lionsgate. Before that, Cinepix was my film school while working, and it was a very rare opportunity because in a way I came into things laterally as opposed to having to really start in film from the bottom up, but I'd certainly worked for a good decade plus going from the bottom up in the theatre.

Ever since I directed *Cube* 3, back in 2002, 2003, I really haven't stopped directing and writing and I've only really produced, I was also directing. So, that's basically how I got into directing movies.

Was that the first franchise that you worked on?

Mind you, *American Psycho* and *Hyper Cube* happened kind of one after the other, I remember I did them in the same year. I worked as producer and writer on *HyperCube*. My first, it's funny, my first full range of sequels, although I was just one of the producers, was actually the prequel to *Nine and a Half Weeks*, called, *The First Nine and a Half Weeks*, and my friend Alex Wright wrote it.

American Psycho 2, I remember Lionsgate approached me with doing that, and there was, it was funny because what I remember, they didn't just approach me to do it; they kind of approached me and already had a script because they had just merged with another company and they were new owners who had some properties, material they were managing.

The first challenge was that they wanted to take an existing script that was written as an original sort of thriller about serial killers, by a really smart writer named Karen Craig. She was the credited writer in American Psycho 2. She originally wrote a very different script that was not an *American Psycho* movie, and the new powers that be kind of pushed us into taking that and adapting it into a movie.

They had me hire Morgan J. Freeman to direct that and he reworked the script a bit too. And, it sort of ended up being much more of a black comedy, and that idea of being black comedy actually came from one of the executives at Lionsgate. It was a good idea because originally the thriller was a very straightforward thriller, and then of course *American Psycho* really works much better as a piece of satire.

Going in, it was a good script, I thought. I think Mila did a good job in the role and so that's the answer to your question; how it started. Lionsgate approached me with a script that they already had that they wanted to turn into *American Psycho* 2, and in hindsight, and it's been a few years now, I'm not sure that was the wisest decision, because really what might have helped, if you really wanted to do an American Psycho sequel was to hire someone to straight up do a sequel to *American Psycho*, not jamming a third-party piece of material in there.

Yeah, and what's funny is that Lionsgate hired me after *Cube Zero*, they actually hired me and I wrote a third *American Psycho* movie that was kind of a Patrick Bateman going through a midlife crisis movie, and that was a really fun script, and they really liked it but it just never got produced because eventually it was just a numbers decision. Creatively they really wanted a true *American Psycho* movie will all the wealth and stuff, and then, when the numbers got crunched, the business model didn't work, it really wasn't working to have—they wanted it done for a lot less money, so it was going to be like; how do you make creatively what we all want, including you, on this very tiny budget?

Did you ever get to meet Brett Easton Ellis

I did, he came to the set in Toronto, he was a really nice guy.

He is an interesting character. Well, I guess he must be to write such an iconic book.

He certainly is. That was a heck of a process, but I really think there was a miss, like we could have done a much better job on a sequel. Again, it goes to the point of what I'm saying, you really have to kind of tune in with the core material and source your sequels and prequels from that. That's why I think there's a miss-step on *American Psycho* 2. It wasn't really the fault of anyone who was involved in the production or the creation of it, it was just that we were kind of in a bizarre business decision from behind the scenes, we were told it has to be sourced actually off of another thing, and kind of retrofitted, retro engineered into *American Psycho* and that was kind of a huge mistake.

But, what can I say? It was either, "Do the movie and have a job, or don't do the movie and nobody gets paid."

Yeah, and I guess compared to lots of other directors and producers, except for like maybe the original *Cube*, you've been involved in the franchise before, so it's not as if you're just jumping in from a blank point.

Yeah, certainly with *Cube,* I was a fan of *Cube* and I really loved the movie, which is when Mike Paseornek at Lionsgate approached me about producing a sequel for *Hyper Cube.* I was thrilled, and then they had hired a really good writer, and a guy who really knew his math and theory behind it all, and Sean Hood who was one of the writers on *HyperCube.* Then of course, once again, it was like Sean had a script that really begged for a $20 million-dollar budget and obviously that wasn't our budget at all. Then, because of scheduling for their slate, it really had to be produced really quickly, so there was really no time to go and really rethink it, and I sort of rewrote it with Lauren McLaughlin, who I'd worked with for years at Lionsgate, and it was the same in many ways, and different in other ways.

Then we had, I hired Andrzej Sekuła who was a great cinematographer to direct it, because he had wanted to be directing and Andrzej was actually the cinematographer in *American Psycho* and he's a really nice man and kind of a visual genius. So, yeah, I think that's why there were some great visual moments in *HyperCube*.

How did you feel after finishing the film? Was it kind of a relief?

Well, any time you finish every movie there's a piece of relief, because filmmaking is a kind of compressed and often stressful scenario even in the best of cases just because it's very physically exhausting, you're working long hours and everything is always to a schedule and a budget, and so there's that relief, but you then sort of miss the people you've been working with closely and stuff.

At the end of the day, I thought *HyperCube* succeeded visually and, in the effects, and music and all the other elements, but I was not in love with the story. I can say that because I was one of the writers, and I thought that we really were kind of rushed into going into production with a script that wasn't by far the best it could be. I kind of had the idea for a prequel or another sequel or something like a third *Cube* movie in the back of my mind, because I was only ever satisfied with *Hyper Cube*.

That's why I came up with *Cube Zero*. Now there were several iterations of *Cube Zero*; it took me a few tries at the script to get to the point where I felt like, "Oh, I get it, I've now gotten to the same world in a way in the first one where I thought the brilliance of *Cube* is when Vincenzo created this becket play in a science fiction genre, and where the philosophy of it and the way the—I guess the existentialism and the philosophy and all that was really at the core of the film, and I thought we'd hit on that in *Cube Zero*. I think that *Cube Zero* was a much more successful story than *Hyper-Cube* because of that.

Yeah, and you must have been pretty happy because it opened to pretty positive reviews and everything, and retrospectively it's still considered a good entry.

Yeah, I know, I love that. That was a lot of work and it took a lot of time. We had, again, a compressed shooting schedule but kind of a really long post because I partnered up with Dennis Berardi and Aaron Weintraub at Mr. X which was a visual effects company in Toronto, and at the same time they were growing and they were starting to do huge films, and understandably so because we weren't paying a lot of money for our visual effects, we didn't have the budget, but they had really huge movies like *Dawn of the Dead* and all sorts of films at the same time. It was like every time those guys had an issue we were the poor cousins waiting.

I'm really happy with *Cube Zero*, and the response it got and I love that fact that it opened at Screamfest, which is a great horror film festival in LA, and it showed in some other festivals and I know Lionsgate was pretty happy with it. And, it was the first film I directed, and then somehow, I was always worried, "Am I ever going to get a second film?" And, I did, and then it was my first movie so I'm pretty happy.

Again, if you told me today to make *Cube Zero* again, I'm sure it would probably be a better movie because I'm, in theory, a more experienced film director now, so I would have shot scenes in a slightly different way, certain scenes and all that. I'm sure the story stuff I would have fixed, but all in all, the things I love about it, which is the story and that we got to the philosophy of things and the questions that the *Cube* universe likes to ask, I'm still pretty happy with that.

Were you hoping there'd be more entries in the franchise?

Well, like I said, I really thought the Cube franchise deserved a third movie after *HyperCube*, but after that and over the years I've been approached, once in a while the guys at Lionsgate will say, "We should make another *Cube* movie," and sort of eye noodle around some ideas, and I know other people come in to pitch them ideas, and it sort of hasn't happened, and I haven't quite—somehow I just never quite found the time to go, "Okay, let me just focus on coming up with a *Cube* idea I can get in there and make happen."

What's funny is, I did at some point, it's funny how these things work in the Zeitgeist so to speak, literally about a month before *Inception* came out, I kind of woke up one day with this idea for a *Cube* movie based on invading people's dreams and then *Inception* comes out the next month, and I'm like, "Well there goes that idea, because obviously now everybody will now think I stole it from *Inception*." In fact, what's really funny is I have a piece of a two-page treatment of a synopsis for a *Cube* based on dreams from ten years before. But, it's nothing like *Inception*, and *Inception* is nothing like it, but I think once you do a part of a franchise and you're dealing with dreams, that's instantly going to be compared.

Yeah, I think even if you showed up on the

internet with that treatment, still, the damage is done and no-one would believe you even against the facts.

Exactly, of course. And, it's okay. They're still making movies and I think every once in a while, I think if the right idea hits, I'd be more than happy to make another *Cube* movie. But, I think the right concept would either have to come to me or be brought to me to do it. I think there's no point in remaking any of the other three movies again. I mean, I had a bit of an idea for kind of a martial arts *Cube*, but I haven't really through that through too far.

And I bet while you're doing everything else, it's kind of always on the back burner.

Yeah, a little bit. A lot of stuff is, so I think how our brains work is sort of like things just sit in the background and kind of semi-boil and something comes up and we remember it and do it.

I guess, I mean, in terms of how you look at it, for you, this might be kind of good, but I guess compared to some people who have directed entries, I mean, obviously now you're in South Africa getting ready to do this Netflix movie, so you're kind of not really just known as the *Cube* guy, if that makes sense?

Yeah, well it's been a while since I've been known as the *Cube* guy. It's interesting, right after *Cube*, Lionsgate hired me to direct—because once the *American Psycho* 3 movie wasn't happening, they hired me to write something else, and they hired me to direct the sequel, to write and direct the sequel to *Stir of Echoes*, and that was *Stir of Echoes: the Homecoming*. What's funny is that was the one starring Rob

Lowe, and I'm working with Rob Lowe now again on this *Christmas In The Wild* movie in South Africa and Zambia.

But, once after those two, I have not really, unless I'm forgetting something, I really haven't done any sequels or prequels or anything like that since *Stir of Echoes* 2 back in 2006.

Like I said, I have nothing against sequels or prequels, it's just that they haven't come together, and it's really not often the first thing I think about when I'm thinking about what I want to do next, but it's not like if something came up or if I suddenly had an idea for something I wouldn't do it. I was approached to—it's funny, I remember I was approached to talk about directing one of the installments of whatever the Ayn Rand book, *Atlas Shrugged* I think. I had a phone call because my agent asked me, "Do a call with the guy behind all that" And, they were really looking for somebody who was all into Ayn Rand and who's a true believer of that, and I'm just not. It's sort of antithetical to how I see life and society so I was obviously not their choice.

Well, yeah. I mean, after the first one the budget for them dropped, didn't they? And, ironically, they actually had to get crowdfunding just to go ahead.

I've heard something like that. It's funny, I was fine when once you go to a place where you're looking for people that really believe the material, you're kind of shrinking the world of the people that can make your movie good. Because, sometimes you need—because rarely can you afford to make a movie that's just for the true believers in any kind of faith-based—in anything. So, it's sometimes great to have somebody who has an outside eye who can bring it to a bigger audience. Anyways, that was one of the few times that I've been approached about sequels and prequels.

When those offers come along, are they something you do consider?

Absolutely, to me, it's about two things; it's about the script, and it's about how is this movie coming together? I mean, you get everybody who works in film and T.V., you get approached about material and then if you don't have a good script or if you can't re-write it or have someone re-write it to be a better script, it's really tough to do because it's a lot of work and if the script doesn't work, no matter what you do with it visually in production, it's just not really going to be the best movie it can be, and it's not going to really work. But really, stuff comes to you and then most of the time people can't put financing together, they expect you to bring movie stars or people to it. Sometimes you do and sometimes you can help, but a lot of the time it just doesn't happen, so it's a combination of material and financing that makes it actually happen.

I told you, I love smart sequels and prequels, because I love seeing how the creator or the writer, how they take it to the next level, take it to the next step. Some of my favourite movies, and I think some of most of our favourite movies are sequels; *The Empire Strikes Back, Aliens*, those are just two that I can name off the top of my head that are instantly at least as good as the original. In some cases, I might argue, better. Part of it is there's no need to introduce as many things. Part of the challenge too, you sometimes have to at least reintroduce some things because you can't assume that the audience for your sequel saw the previous film, and that's a bit of a challenge; you've got to really figure out how to put exposition in there without boring the people who have seen the original. Stuff like that.

Like, you can introduce things in the beginning, but at some point, people kind of realize it isn't there anymore, and you have to keep moving things forward. At a certain point, you can introduce a new element here and there to surprise them, but then, you shouldn't do it too soon or too late. Then, you've got to wrap it up and there's a finesse to be had when handling material like that.

Do you have any thoughts about the whole kind of lore and how people eat it up and why it happens?

I think part of it today, with the advent of social media, that you really are in a way in-touch with your audience more, especially the genre audience, especially with franchises ... and so in a way you can do a lot. If you're going to plan a sequel do your research and really find out what people want, or what they think they want, which isn't always the best thing either. Kind of what they expect, what they don't expect, what they love, what they hate. But again, as a writer think what do people want when you write that, because sometimes what people want is to be surprised, so you can't just go by what they're telling you right then, but it's really, that is to me the big difference between making sequels and prequels now versus ten years ago and earlier.

What have you got in the pipeline, is it all focusing on then?

I finished shooting a film called, *Abduction* in China and Vietnam. It's kind of this Roger Corman executive produced alien abduction martial arts movie with Scott Atkins and Andy On and a woman named Truong Ngoc Anh (aka TNA) from Vietnam, and so we're still in kind of post-production for that, while I'm in prep for *Christmas In The Wild.*

Christmas In The Wild is a really cool film, I think it's really going to be helpful to the whole plight of endangered species, especially elephants in Africa. It's also a Christmas movie, which is kind of a fun combination and it's a romance with Rob Lowe and Kristin Davis, so it's a very different movie than the genre stuff; more action-thriller-horror movie that I've done.

And, I like going back and forth, I do both. I do the Netflix Hallmark Christmas movie thing and romances and romantic comedies and then of course, but a lot of, half if not more of what I do is the action thriller stuff, and that's great. I love going back and forth because at some point, even though I love action movies and thrillers and horror, I think if you were to do that continuously in a row, you kind of almost get stale, and you start falling back on old tricks and you don't really want to do that as any kind of creator material.

So, I'm grateful for the opportunity because a lot of people in this business get boxed into a box and that's all people see you as and it's boring as hell. Which is fascinating to me because in the theatre, people rarely I found did that. Nobody would go, "You're the guy who directs Shakespeare, but can you also do a Neil Simon play," it was understood that if you could do one, you could probably do the other.

But yeah, *Christmas In The Wild* is my next project, and then after that, nothing is for sure, there's a film that we're putting the financing together for and trying to cast that's called *Helios*, it's the disaster movie about a solar flare storm coming to earth, and that would be more than likely to happen in 2019, but that's about it.

That would be a bigger budget one.

I guess so, you just never know. We'll see how it all comes together.

INTERVIEW ADAM MARCUS

"I wanted filmmakers that came after to me to be able to make things that they were excited about, and that they had this whole new canvas to paint on."

Selected Filmography:

Jason Goes To Hell: The Final Friday
Let It Snow
Conspiracy
Texas Chainsaw Massacre 3D
Secret Santa

How did you get started in film and where did the original interest come from?

Okay. So, for me everything started when I was a little kid. My best friend was a kid called Mike Cunningham, who happened to be Sean Cunningham's son. So, I really was constantly underfoot with the Cunninghams. Sean was in many ways a cinematic father for me. I would do anything just to help out with anything that he was working on. I fell in love with movies, especially the kind of movies that he was making. I was in the editing room with Susan Cunningham, his wife working on *Spring Break*, which was a totally inappropriate movie for me to be around when I was 13. I was there for *Friday the 13th*, the original, and I just fell in love with production and movies and by the time I was 15 I had completed my first two theatrical companies and in fact Sean was very helpful in the monetising of the first company. And the first of those companies turning a profit was what enabled me to go to NYU Film School.

I had been obsessed with horror since I was a very small child. In fact, the *Evil Dead* was a big turning point for me because I grew up in Westport Connecticut and Manhattan, between my mom and dad, and for the movie *Evil Dead* everybody was buzzing about it. I was obsessed with going to see it, but we couldn't find a theatre that would show it. I had a buddy in Manhattan who was able to get me a bootleg copy of it on VHS. This is before bootleg copies were readily available, it was a big deal. We huddled together in my friend's basement and watched *Evil Dead*. That was the movie that truly made me feel like "I can do this" because it is super low budget, super scrappy, I knew the origins: a bunch of friends that went to college together and believed in each other. Between *Friday the 13th* and *Evil Dead* is where my love of genre came from, and my love of by any means necessary being a film maker. It was the match that lit my fuse.

When I went to NYU I won best picture for a romantic comedy I made. I got two job offers, one to write for Season 2 of *Twin Peaks*, and the other was from Sean Cunningham to come to Los Angeles and be his slave for a year and he would give me my shot. I could not have jumped on a plane quicker to go meet Sean. I had 300 bucks in my pocket and no driver's license, because I was living in New York. Once I got to LA I stayed with a couple of friends but lived in my car for quite a bit of time. It was a 63 VW Bug, canary yellow, like Kevin Bacon drives in *Footloose*. I thought that was really cool because Kevin Bacon was in *Friday the 13th.* I had a copy of a screenplay that my best friend from college, Dean Lorey, had been working on for years. It was the movie I wanted to make my directorial debut with, a movie called *Johnny Zombie.*

I started talking to different companies around LA about the project, I didn't bring it up to Sean because I was his slave. I knew if I talked to enough people and if I talked to Noel about the people I was talking to, Sean would get interested. He saw the script on my desk, asked me what it was, and I told him it's the first feature I want to direct. He read it in 90 minutes. He said, "I hate this script, but I love the title, I'm going to give you 1.5 million dollars to shoot it in Connecticut." But he wanted me to get another writer. I told him that I wasn't going to sell it to him, and he couldn't believe the balls on me to say that, and to this day I still don't believe I said that. I said "Dean Lorey is an amazing writer, I believe in him. Why don't you fly him to LA, put him up in a hotel for 6 weeks and give him a chance for a rewrite. If he can't do the rewrites you want then get someone else." Dean came to LA, and rewrote the script in 6 weeks.

Once it was done, Sean loved the project. One of the things I did as a kid, because of my theatre background, was doing readings. We put together casts of remarkable actors to put together these table reads, and Sean invited executives from studios to come and watch the readings. It was genius because the executives tend to never read, it's not what they do. Our feeling was if they're not going to read let's read it for them. The first person to read for

Johnny Zombie was Adam Sandler who went to NYU the same time I did. We got New Line and Disney into it, they loved it and wanted the script. Disney had deeper pockets, which Sean loved, and they ended up buying the film.

The problem was we had written this subversive R-rated horror comedy and Disney was never going to make that. They wanted to get rid of the Zombie, that was their only note. "Can he seem less dead and more tired." My response was that this was not the movie I want to make.

I went back to Sean and said "I set up the movie with Disney, get someone else to direct it, this isn't what I want to do. Get me something else to direct." He did. He told me Paramount was selling off the rights to New Line for the *Friday the 13th* franchise. At that point he said, "if you can get that fucking mask out of the movie, I'll let you write and direct the film." And I said okay. Three days later I brought him a treatment that would become *Jason Goes To Hell: The Final Friday*. I had just turned 22 when he offered me that project.

That's remarkably young to be offered that level of responsibility, working on something so iconic.

Yeah, I was 23 when I shot the film. The youngest writer/ director ever to be hired by a movie studio.

And since you worked with Sean you were familiar with the franchise as it progressed and developed with each installment?

Oh yeah, I saw each of them in the theatre. At that point, I owned them all but *Part 8*, I had to buy a copy of that when we were working on the film.

Was it difficult to blow Jason up? For a while it hints at being the last film in the franchise.

Sean now claims in a YouTube video that me saying that he said to get rid of the mask is a fucking lie. He said that. My response to that has always been "Okay, hang on a sec. You're saying, according to you, Sean, that a 22-year-old film student said "I'm going to blow up the mask in a *Friday the 13th* movie, get rid of the mask, and you said okay?!" A 22-year-old is telling a 50 plus Sean Cunningham what he is going to do with the franchise. Either I'm the most powerful 22-year-old on planet Earth and he's a eunuch, or he told me to get rid of a hockey mask and he's the liar. It's one or the other, and I'll take either one!

For me, I knew if I get rid of Jason Voorhees in a *Friday the 13th* film, I'm toast. The audience is going to hate me and kill me, because so would I. My response to that is he wants me to get rid of the hockey mask, he didn't say get rid of Jason. You have to remember Sean Cunningham only made the first movie. He was the rights owner for the other movies. He likes to run around saying how he guided the franchise, Frank Mancuso Jr who I also worked for at one point, guided that franchise. Sean made a movie about a mom killing teenagers in revenge for her dead son. That's the movie Sean made. He didn't make a movie about a guy with a hockey mask. His protege Steve Miner, perfect film maker, made one about a potato sack wearing Jason, that I think is the scariest of the Jasons, then introduced the hockey mask in *Part 3*.

I knew, okay, I wasn't getting rid of Jason, that's crazy. I thought how cool it would be if we gave Jason more of a mythology. Here's the thing, by *Part 8* of the franchise, look at the loop de loops Paramount was doing to keep people interested in the character. Nobody ever thinks about if you're writing / directing one of the movies, eventually the

Mexican wrestler in the hockey mask isn't interesting anymore. How many machete kills are interesting to watch?

Let's be honest, by *Jaws 4* no one wanted to see the shark anymore, they had to make it more complicated. By *Part 6*, which is my favourite movie of the franchise; beautifully directed, hilarious writing — the first *Friday the 13th* had a generous sense of humour, but they turned Jason into a zombie. *Part 6* stars zombie Jason, *Part 7* a psychic teenager like Carrie versus Jason, *Part 8*, they're like "I know! Let's put him against the city of New York." The problem was the diminishing returns at the box office for Paramount meant they were making them for less and less money.

It's called *Jason Takes Manhattan*, it should be called Jason Takes a Boat Ride. He takes a boat for 60 minutes, and he's in New York for 28 minutes and any action they get is in Canada. There he is in lovely Montreal and anyone from New York recognises that, and they have that one scene in Times Square. My feeling is this, and I think it's why the Freddy movies started to have a diminishing return as well, and its why *New Nightmare* is so interesting is because he brought back the heroine. I think the hero is only is as interesting as the villain, and I think that works in reverse, the villain is only as interesting as the hero. And Tommy Jarvis was a complicated and interesting hero. In *Part 5* he's the new Jason for God's sake, and that gets thrown out the window for *Part 6*.

The franchise had this legacy of throwing stuff out the window to make the next part work. For my film, I originally wanted it to be the last entry in the chapter between Tommy and Jason. I wanted to make a movie much more about Jason's origins and have Tommy get rid of Jason Voorhees forever. We were wondering, how do we send this guy away from our plain forever.

I started to think from a real-life perspective: you had this murderer from a small town in New Jersey, the Cropsey killer basically, who has murdered over 100 people in a decade. That's no longer a local law enforcement problem that's a serial killer. You have to bring in the FBI. The FBI would bring in a task force for a guy who killed this many people, and they would create a sting. The opening of the movie comes directly from that idea. I love it when people say I'm shoe-horning it in because the evidence is all over the movie. My obsession with *Evil Dead* is peaked at this point, and I got to hang out the set of *Army of Darkness*, I got to meet Sam Raimi and hang out with him and it was amazing.

I was working on the Jason script at that point and realised I had a real problem: you've got this character who was killed decades earlier still looks like a little boy coming out of the lake. It's not seen from Alice's eyes, she's not aware of whose attacking her. In the hospital, she asks "what about the boy". A boy that is living at the bottom of Crystal Lake is waiting for passing by canoes. Okay, so that means that little boy is in some ways a monster. Then in *Part* 2, somehow the little boy who was dead and is Pamela Voorhees' special son, has learned to read a map, find an address, do all kinds of research on how to find Alice, and oh, by the way, in a short period of time, he is now somehow a grown man. The other thing is he has found a great package of clothing to wear, grow a couple of feet, can drive to a house and then takes her remains and his mother's head to Crystal Lake to put them on his shrine. Who helped him move the body?

Back at Crystal Lake, now you've got a character whose sustained more damage than anyone over the next few movies. Chopped up, beaten, stabbed, over and over until finally Tommy Jarvis kills this thing. A lot of people go, it's *Part 6*, now he becomes zombie Jason. I'm sorry guys, there's something to making this character survive and stay quite efficient even though he's been hacked to pieces by *Part 4*. In *Part 6* he is resurrected by a bolt of lightning, *Part 7* he's attacked by a psychic, In *Part 8* he ends up in toxic waste and turns into a little boy. Let's say I take all of this as gospel, what is the explanation for Jason Voorhees? That's when I met Sam Raimi, I said "Wait a second, can I borrow the Necronomicon?"

I knew that New Line could never let me make a mash up of the two franchises because they didn't own the rights. There were so many things like the Freddy Glove they did own the rights to. I asked Sam if I could borrow the book and we can make our own version of the dagger. That's why the book is in Pamela Voorhees' house, I thought, let's say she makes a deal with the darkness, she reads the book because she would do anything to have her Jason back, and resurrects him as this monster from hell. Now Jason being pulled back from hell means he is being called back home. It's why the earth opens up and drags him down. People say it's not true – there's a scene where she's reading from the book! It's not a mistake. I had to actively go get the book. It was to give some sense of logic that Jason is this monster. Freddy has always been that, he can do whatever he wants because he can engineer dreams. So what *Jason Goes to Hell* did was give him some magic, it's about this creature that is Jason Voorhees rather than just this rotting flesh.

After all of these years it's easy to tell that it was a labour of love. So how did you hide the *Evil Dead* reference for copyright issues?

As long as Sam gave me the thumbs up and he did, he gave me the book in a zip-locked bag, as long as we could have that there and didn't mention the *Evil Dead* inside the movie I'm safe. All it ends up looking like is I'm doing a homage to a great horror film, which I was. There was a ton of homages in the movie, the dagger is the only thing that can kill Jason Voorhees.

You think people wouldn't question you if you directed the film.

It's the birth of the internet that made all this fun possible. Everyone has their own mythology of how the movies got built and that's what they stick with. I totally understand the people that say why would you take away the hockey mask. I didn't, I took it away for 65 minutes of running time. The rest of the movie is hockey mask, it comes back at the end. In every screening I did prior to the release, when Jason burst up from the floorboards at the end of the film people went berserk. Other people say I didn't follow my own rules because he wasn't reborn, he was the Jason at the beginning of the film again, my response is he comes back through a dead woman's body, he doesn't come back entirely. Had he been born through the baby, absolutely, then they would be able to say he should look like young Jason and I would agree.

You know, as a creator of material, when you're crafting something, rewriting every little detail, none of this stuff is happenstance, you agonise over every detail, it's what writers and directors do. I'm 22 years old and I'm agonising over every page of this script, I cared, I cared so tremendously, today I still care. Whenever I take someone through the chronology of the 8 movies before my film, everyone always goes "Oh, yeah that is weird. Why are all those jumps in logic okay." And if you say Jason is part of the *Evil Dead* universe, it covers it all. Like *Rogue One*, the reason for that film existing is every *Star Wars* fan, myself included, saying "They left a hole in the death star to blow it up? Ridiculous." *Rogue One* comes along and that solves that problem.

That's what I love. A service to the fans as much as a creative decision.

I was a huge fan of the movies and the characters. It's like giving *Jaws* a personality. So, when I made the movie, I wasn't making it as a casual observer, I was making it a someone who was involved in the franchise because I was attached to it in a weird way. I was a fan, I was making this film, it was made for the fans by the fan. It's a luxury for horror movies, especially in the early 90s, you had people making these films that had grown up watching these films. I was making a movie that for me as a fan, would help all this other stuff makes sense.

Jason Goes to Hell is as bat shit crazy as it is, that if people remove themselves from the idea of a "Jason Voorhees movie", you say do you like the acting? Characters? Writing? Kills? Then I go, "So what's the problem! The Hockey Mask, that you got 6 films of nothing but hockey mask, and that's the problem? Do you want another hockey mask or do you want a movie with something else on its mind? That's the issue with mainstream horror because it's hard to make something with a brain in its head because horror fans are so dogmatic that they won't allow any room for horror fans to make art.

I know some people hate Rob Zombie's *Halloween*, but my response to it was do I like them more than the original movies? No, I don't. Do I think Rob Zombie is a remarkable filmmaker with an incredibly specific voice? Yes. Do I think if horror fans want pretty things they have to be more inclusive of ideas that might rattle their cages a little? Yeah. Horror movies are meant to be the most cage shaking movies, and a lot of the time people want the same old same old. That sucks, as a child I wanted things that would rock my world every time. With the franchise characters, you look at things like *Freddy's Dead* and he becomes a joke.

He becomes truly a punchline in that film. I didn't want Jason to be a punchline; I wanted Jason to—look, I'm no fool. I knew it would never be the final Friday, I knew they would make *Freddy vs. Jason*, I knew all of that stuff would happen, so for me, I wanted filmmakers that came after to me to be able to make things that they were excited about, and have this whole new canvas they could paint on.

And you knew it wouldn't be the final film, and there was probably the talks of *Freddy vs. Jason* and then *another* sequel?

Yes. Here's the thing, the theme with the gloves at the end of the movie, that is 100%, I'm the guy who came up with that, my roommates and I were all hanging out in our apartment, we're trying to figure out stuff to do for the movie. So the three of us were all joking about the different cool Easter eggs we could put in the movie before there were such a thing as Easter eggs. We were coming up with all these different cool things we can pace, and I said, "Wait a second, doesn't Freddy, isn't Freddy 100% by New Line, they own that franchise outright?" And they're like, "Yeah." I said, "Okay, they just killed Freddy, Freddy is dead, it just happened, Freddy is in hell already, so who better to drag Jason's last remains to hell than Freddy Kruger?" And, my roommate is like, "That's fucking awesome!" And I called Mark Ordesky and Mike De Luca, got them on the phone, and said, "Can I have Freddy's glove?" And the first response was, "What do you want it for?" And I told them what I wanted the ending moment to be, and they were like, "Abso-freaking-lutely. Absolutely."

It was hilarious because they showed up to set with Freddy's glove in a locked case, it was amazing. It was actually Robert Shaye's personal version of the glove that we were allowed to use, and that's how that scene got in the film. But again, it wasn't New Line dictating that, they just didn't do it. In fact, I had to go to court, I had to give a deposition that that fact at one point because there was a writer trying to sue New Line and there was all this nonsense. Saying that he had pitched this to New Line and New Line told me and I was like, "No!" And so I gave a deposition and we beat this guy in court over it.

But, again, I wanted there to be this great mash-up, and then when the first audience, our very first test screening, that moment comes up at the end of the film where Freddy pulls Jason's mask into hell, the audience went out of their minds. I've never seen anything like it in my life actually. I remember all the New Line executives were high-fiving in the back of the theatre, because they knew *Freddy vs. Jason* is going to be huge. And they were right.

What happened after the film was released, how did you cope with it and the reception, how did affect your career moving forward?

Here's the interesting thing, the thing that happened with the movie, and again, people forget, there was no Internet back then, there was no chat rooms, there was nobody talking about the movie in that way. So, the response to the film, while I know there were a lot of people that were just pissed off, that didn't come back to me right away, it just didn't. I had a multiple picture deal at New Line that was going on. I met with Robert De Niro's company in New York, and I met with Francis Ford Coppola here in L.A. Those were my meetings right after the movie happened.

So, doors were opening, which was great. The problem was, Ted Turner bought New Line almost immediately, and killed all horror at New Line, literally everything died. I had a multiple picture deal that died. Right after that, I started getting offered a ton of horror sequels, and I just went, "I don't want to be this guy. I don't want to be this filmmaker, I just don't. I don't want to be a guy who has a part number after every movie he makes. I knew guys like that, I knew a lot of guys like that. I got offered *Pumpkinhead* 2. The reason I wouldn't do *Pumpkinhead* 2 was because the movie took place in the bayou— that was the story. At that time, they would not let me write black characters. I felt the screenplay needed a rewrite and they would not let me write black characters.

As in write them into the script, or as in a politically correct view, wouldn't let you voice them way?

It was, first off, it didn't make sense to me; you're making movies at the bayou, yet you're not going to have black characters in the film? Second, quote unquote, black does not sell overseas. I was infuriated by that, I thought that was so awful, I was like, "No, not going to do this." By the way, the proof of them offering this movie to me is that I got Bill Dill the job.

They said something about the witch, the witch herself was white, and I was like, "This voodoo which woman living in the bayou and she's white?" What movie are you guys telling? I said, "Can't we just at least make that character African-American?" And they were like, "No, we've already chosen somebody for that character and they've done the make-up already." And again, KNB Effects did the make up on the movie, KNB wanted me to do this—I'm telling you, I was actually interested in *Pumpkinhead* 2, because I felt like it was a franchise that hadn't been played out. It was like, "Okay, maybe we can create something new and fresh and interesting with this. Every step of the way, the excuses to not make this movie inclusive drove me absolutely berserk.

I said, "No, not going to do this. Thanks, I'm good." That was the problem, there were these movies...I just felt like we had been offered several *Leprechaun* films, I don't want to make a *Leprechaun* movie; I just don't. Look, there's no snob factor to it, but once you've been to Jason, going down the scale of great serial killer franchises just felt like this is going to be diminishing returns; I'm not interested.

However, when *Texas Chainsaw* came along, my wife and I were like, "Okay, this is something we'll do, this is exciting." But, I've got to tell you, from a career standpoint, yeah, I was really young and I didn't want to get put in a box, so the very next film I made, I'd set up several projects and studios. I had a movie at Warner Bros., I had a movie at Paramount, I had set up a bunch of films and they were original movies which is great. So, at least I had original stuff going on.

I went back to New York and my brother and I put together a movie called, *Let it Snow*, that was a huge Sundance hit, that was a hit all over the world actually. We had festival oncoming from every direction, and it started actually getting a career in television, we started writing for TV, which then actually just brought me back into features and I started writing for Fox Studios.

I mean, here's the thing, the reception of *Jason Goes to Hell* has actually been more interesting later in my career, now in particular, because people are ranting, raving and foaming at the mouth about the movie. "I hate that fucking movie, you killed my childhood." Or, there's this new resurgence of love for the movie that's been kind of surprising. I did not expect it. Because this year is the 25th anniversary of the film. I'm going to a bunch of screenings, I've been going to screenings for the movie, it was just shown in Chicago two weeks ago.

The audience goes out of their minds for the movie, and they love the movie. I'm meeting all these people who are like, "It was my first *Friday the 13th* in the theatre, and I love this film." Just two years ago I started a new production company with my wife, Debra, and my best friend and my partner, Bryan Sexton. And, we're making, the name of the company, Skeleton Crew, and we're making a lot of new horror films.

I just made a film called *Secret Santa* that's been burning up the festival circuit, we were actually just at Glasgow Fright Fest a couple of months ago. We're doing that, and we just got picked up with the UK distributor, and the movie is getting just tons of critical love and festival love. A lot of that is riding on the back of *Jason Goes to Hell* and *Texas Chainsaw*. Look, here's the thing that's great about these franchises, and the reason why I am so blessed to have had Sean Cunningham in my life and to have him as a cinematic father and as a producer.

By the way, Sean Cunningham is a remarkable producer. He's one of those guys who can get twenty bucks out of a nickel, he's that guy. Why I'm blessed for this is, when I think about all the great films that have come out in the last 25 years, and I mean, masterpieces that are not talked about, that no one ever brings up, that people have literally just forgotten because we're so inundated with media. On the first night, on the night *Jason Goes to Hell* came out, I had seen the movie so many times at that point, and I just needed a break, especially a week before the movie, every night I was in the back for *Jason Goes to Hell*, we watched the film. So, the night the movie came out, I walked into a theatre, into a multiplex. I paid for *Jason Goes to Hell* because I wanted my movie to get as much money as possible, but I walked into *Searching for Bobby Fischer*, have you ever seen it?

No, I haven't.

It is a masterpiece. Steven Zaillian wrote and directed it,

the guy who wrote Schindler's list. Joe Mantegna, Ben Kingsley, Joan Allen, it's an incredible film, an incredible, incredible film. It opened the same night as my movie. Now, it made almost no money, it got nothing but rave reviews, it's just across the board, everybody loved the film. No-one talks about *Searching for Bobby Fisher*, and it's a masterpiece, it's an extraordinary movie. But, people are still debating *Jason Goes to Hell* 25 years later. That as a filmmaker, that's the coolest thing in the world; whether people love it, whether people hate it, whether they debate about it, whatever it is, the fact that the fans who are—look, horror fans are the most rabid and the best fans on the planet, they just are. They are loyal to these movies to the end.

By the way, even the ones they don't like, they're loyal to in their own weird way. *Halloween 3: Season of the Witch* gets more ink, that movie gets so much ink, and it's the most debated movie of that franchise, because that's a movie where there is no Michael Myers, he's just not in the movie. But of course, *Halloween* 3 is closest to what John Carpenter wanted to do with *Halloween* to begin with, which was, he didn't want to tell the story of Michael Myers, he wanted to movies about *Halloween*, that's what he wanted to do.

For me, the fact that the fans keep these movies alive, that they keep talking about them, the truth is, I'm sure you've heard, they're making a documentary about *Jason Goes to Hell* right now. That's crazy! And kind of awesome. Honestly, the movie has affected my career in that it's made me come back to horror, because I love horror. It is my first love. So, the whole *Jason Goes to Hell* phenomenon helped to make that happen. It's part of the reason we got *Texas Chainsaw*, it's part of the reason we got to write that film. I can't bemoan my time with Jason, it's actually one of my happiest memories, and it is something that I think in its own weird way has buoyed my career, where a lot of people just kind of fall off, a lot of horror filmmakers just sort of disappear.

I will not go gently into that dark night, no way. I'm coming with my hockey mask.

There's been a resurgence recently, because there was that *Friday the 13th* video game, they did a lot of the footage for. Oddly enough the other day I was just playing this *Friday the 13th* puzzle game on my phone. That's really fun. So it's still going strong and I'm sure they're probably finally working on a reboot somewhere.

I'm sure they are. They've got to figure out this rights situation which is a mess. It's a mess.

What was your feelings on *Freddy vs. Jason* then *Jason X* and then the reboot?

Here's the thing; I think *Freddy versus Jason*; do you remember that scene in *Freddy vs. Jason* when Jason is literally taking a nap on the couch and all the kids are discussing how they're going to get rid of Freddy and Jason? That scene to me, I laughed out loud in the theatre. The reason I laughed out loud is, I went, "Oh my God, I think someone just put a microphone in the office with all the executives when they were actually trying to figure out how to make this plot work. It sounded like teenagers saying the lines of film executives about, "How do we break this story? Because we have no idea how to get rid of these two characters."

Freddy vs. Jason could have been so epic and I think instead, it's a beautifully shot movie, the kills are terrific, they got a great looking cast of actors, but ultimately it just— they did the least they could do to service the fans but didn't create a movie that I would go back to over and over again, and I wish they had, because I want that movie. I think it could have been far more exciting, far more kick-ass, and for me it became kind of a wrestling match. I like a little more story in my story, you know? That to me I felt was a bit of a missed opportunity, even though it's incredibly well done, everybody involved with that movie did their job, and did it admirably, but it just feels safe. And for a movie that's about the two worst guys ever put on screen, to feel safe, feels like a missed opportunity.

That's *Freddy vs. Jason*. *Jason X*, look, they needed to keep the rights where they were. They had to make a movie, they had no choice, they had to make a movie. I think that *Jason X* kind of follows in the tradition with the Paramount movies. I always love when people go New Line, no, no, eventually Paramount would have shot Jason in his face, they had run out of stuff to do with it. Psychic girl sitting out in space, so there were a lot of franchises that started sending horror into space. I get the reason why, I think again, there were really cool ideas in *Jason X*, I think the script.... I got to read the original script, it's a better script than it was a movie. Todd Farmer did a really good job on that script. I just think the budget limitations and all that, it kept the movie from being what it could have been. But, do I think there's cool stuff in that movie? Absolutely I do, and I have watched that movie several times.

For me, the reboot, I am not a fan. I love Marcus, I think Marcus Nispel is a terrific guy, he's a really cool filmmaker, but I am not a big fan of the reboot, I'm really not. It feels to me like the cliffs notes version of the *Friday the 13th* franchise. It feels rushed. There's stuff in it that I think is so badass and cool, but honestly, it really does feel like *Part 1* through 4 shoved into one film, I find it to be a very weird film. And, I love Marcus' reboot of *Texas Chainsaw*. I think that's a terrific movie and I'm a huge fan of the original, and

I honour Toby like nobody else. The guy is—forget about legend, just a terrific film voice. But no. Have you seen *Never Hike Alone*?

I think that's a really clever way to take on the Jason character. It's not a feature, it's a shorter film but I think what he did with that movie is really smart, I think the mono a mono version of Jason is really clever and scary. For me I think that the fans are actually doing a great service to Voorhees by creating these little movies that are actually more frightening.

By the way, I didn't get to say earlier, but I will put it on record; I wanted Tommy Jarvis to be the lead of *Jason Goes to Hell*. I couldn't have him. Because New Line didn't buy Tommy Jarvis, they bought Jason. We didn't own for the Friday the 13th name, that's why none of the New Line Movies are called Friday the 13th, and they did not own any of the material from those movies. They own Jason Voorhees and Crystal Lake, that's what they owned. Furthering sort of the complications with all these 'rights issues' that are splintered and all over the place, and so you know so Steven Freeman was born out of Tommy Jarvis, who was my version of Tommy Jarvis, but that's who the character was supposed to be, so just wanted to put that on the record.

If you count the inspiration of Freddy Kruger in the franchise you kind of more than most people had an influence across the biggest franchises in horror.

Yeah, again I feel really, really lucky too. I will say this, when it comes to *Texas Chainsaw*, our original script for that movie – Debra and I – first off, we went up against 17 writers and writing teams to win that job, so there were 17 groups of writers that did for the *Texas Chainsaw* job. We won that job in part because the producers really loved us, in part because we walked into our first meeting about the movie and we brought the first eleven pages of the screenplay with us and the full treatment that we had written and we'd only written it in about two weeks from the time that we were told we were coming into this meeting, because we really loved the idea of doing this movie.

The one thing I'll say about *Texas Chainsaw* because I know it's the biggest phantom point and I agree with it; so Debra and I were hired to write a twenty million dollar movie and they ended up making an eight million dollar movie, so our screenplay for *Texas Chainsaw* is huge. I mean it is such a blood bath; there are so many kills in this movie, and spectacular ones because we knew it was going to be in 3D and we were going to shoot it in 3D and it wasn't a conversion, and so we wrote these – I mean the scene at the carnival was; normally a carnival of death and they couldn't shoot it.

When they went to go and make the movie they couldn't shoot it because they just didn't have the money anymore. They were virtually going to do a twenty-million-dollar show. The other thing; the big complaint from the fans is the timeline and how the movie takes place literally as the first film ends which is what we wanted it... that was the whole idea; was we wanted it connected immediately to the original film. That was what we wanted and then the producers were like, "Great we can take the last five minutes of Toby's movie and can work those images to make them 3D."

Like yeah, that's great because again, my response was, "Okay let's take this logically. Sally escapes; she gets in the truck, she gets away. The first place she is going to is the police and the police are going to come right back to that house" and I was like, "I want to know what happens at that house. I want to see the stand-off between the Sawyers and the local PD; that's an interesting shot." So that's what really takes place.

Of course, you know the two local fields of baby Sawyer in the house and twenty years later she has no idea that she's part of this family and she gets a letter from her grandmother saying, "You're inheriting my fortune. Come to Texas." Okay. Here's the thing: the minute that fucking cell phone comes out in that movie; the bad cop doing that whole cell phone scene; it ruined the film. It probably was a good sequence. It was a well-done sequence, but where I'm sorry, that girl in that truck is not forty years old. She's twenty and it... the movie jumps the shark at that point. I mean it doesn't make any goddamn sense.

Debra and I wrote a movie that was supposed to take place in 1993 and that number is very significant to me because that's the undertaking of how it was released so I was actually kind of... it was actually... I even had a note in one of the drafts that in the local movie theatres they can have *Jason Goes to Hell* playing it behind them so we had our timeline exact and correct. We knew exactly what our timeline was. When the producers went down to make the movie and when the director who looked... John was obviously an accounted filmmaker, but the problem is I don't think he gives a shit about horror movies and he made a movie where he's just a man.

Dude, okay, in our original ending scene Leatherface is surrounded by a dozen of these guys who have helped murder his family in what ends up becoming the slaughterhouse. So he's surrounded by twelve guys. When he gets hold of his chainsaw he kills twelve people in that scene. He killed the local bully and his assistant; that's it. Two people; what? He's Leatherface. He's Frankenstein's monster. How do you have two guys take him down? We had a dozen guys. So for me you know I've...boy, that is a script. By the way that script has gotten Debra and I other jobs. I mean it's one of our favourite things we've ever written and we even had that story on Leatherface, we had his origin story in there, we had like really cool stuff. When Toby Hooper read our script he called us to congratulate us.

Toby loved the screenplay. He was like, "This is the best true sequel for my first movie." He loved the sequel, and when they made the movie, I wish they had made the movie with someone who for me felt like a fan. He didn't feel like a fan of the franchise and again, they short-cheated every scene. We had a scene in *Texas Chainsaw* where Leatherface shows up to that slaughterhouse and in Texas; this is so barbaric; in Texas the slaughterhouse; the slaughterhouses are right next to the cattle farms. So these cows are smelling their own death their whole lives so when Leatherface shows up to the you know to the... to where they're at we had the cattle stampede and so there was this moment where Leatherface is walking through a herd of stampeding cattle with the chainsaw revving.

I'm like, "There's your poster. That's the movie." Like sharing parts of these long-horned steers running around Leatherface with his chainsaw; that's' a poster. So you know we wrote a movie that was really badass and in a lot of ways it kind of got littered and they fucked up the timeline and that timeline is not in our script. There are no cell phones in our movie. In fact there's walkie-talkies all over the movie because there weren't cell phones.

That first script is a badass script and by the way another thing that was in there: the kids don't pick up the hitchhiker. They don't pick up the hitchhiker. They don't drive the hitchhiker up to grandma's house and then leave the hitchhiker in the house so he can steal from them. There were traces that were made in that final movie that I just go, "I don't know want you guys were thinking." And look, I agree with the fans. I was pissed about the same things they were pissed about. Of course when your name is there as the writer of the movie people blame you and I was like, "No, no, no, no. It's a show. I didn't want anybody to watch... did you read the script? Did you get our draft?" It bears no resemblance.

What are you doing these days now just kind of running the production company with your wife and mainly writing?

I'm actually producing more and directing more than anything else right now. My wife and I wrote; I directed and produced *Secret Santa* with my brother Ryan so *Secret Santa* is the new thing out, but no we've got about six films that are all in development around the company. One is a big movie that I can't talk about yet because we're about to announce, but it's a really big film that we're doing. It's got A-list talent attached and then I'm doing another; I'm doing a thriller later this year called *The Harvest* which is kind of a passion project of mine that's scary as hell, but it's applauded. It's kind of not too similar from *A History of Violence*. It's that kind of show.

So it's yeah, it's a knack in that area so no, I'm actually I am doing a ton and I've got to tell you that part of the reason... *Texas Chainsaw* is actually a big part of the reason why I created the production company with my partners because the three of us had been making so many films and my partner Bryan's producer was trying to add movies. The three of us were so tired of making films for people who always say that they know better than you and then they make decisions like, "Let's put a cell phone in the middle of the movie that's supposed to take place in 1993."

And so I kind of went, "You know what do we do with all of this stuff and if I'm going to get booed for something I'm happy to take it away. I'm, happy if somebody doesn't like something in the movie, but I want it to be something I did, not something that a studio executive said that this is the way it's going to go or some producer had it re-written and re-written back. I also want to work with people that I want to work with, and that's been the coolest thing about Skeleton Crew is that I'm working with Robert Kurtzman again and Robert did all the effects in *Secret Santa* for me and then he came on as the executive producer and he shot second camera on the movie. I got Robert Kurtzman edging the camera effects whose made over four hundred movies, who in the middle of *Secret Santa* he walks up to me; we were shooting all night and he said, "Hey Adam, I want to thank you." I said, "For what man? I'm the one who should be thanking you." He goes, "No man." He goes, "This is the best experience I've had in a decade." He's like, "This is what movie making is."

And you know *Secret Santa* was made with a crew of six people and a cast of twenty and it's the movie that I am more proud of than anything else I've ever made. I shot the movie in eleven days or eleven nights and it's because it's the kind of movie making that I fell in love with when I watched the first *Evil Dead*. It's making things because you really believe in them. It's making the things for people that you love so that the job becomes like going camping. It's like the best job in the world.

Now I am more excited and happier as a film maker than I've ever been in my life. Debra and I had a film called *Momentum* that came back a couple of years ago with Morgan Freeman and Olga Kurylenko and James Purefoy which is kind of an action thriller. We wrote that yeah and again, you know we've had the kind of career where I've been writing for the last twenty-seven years and I've got literally scripts of every studio in town sitting on shelves and that's the life of a screen writer. You know you hopefully get paid to write a lot of stuff. Most of it gets left sitting on shelves. People think that goes right into production – nah. Our film *Momentum*; the one that I was mentioning with James Purefoy and Morgan Freeman; that movie took twenty years to get to the screen and that's normal. You know that these things... it takes a long time for these movies to just play and find their home, but again with Skeleton Crew the great thing is anything I want to do I go and do and that's the best freedom in the world. It's amazing.

I've only taken one job in my life to pay bills and I regretted it every fucking second. I really did because there are much easier ways to make a living in this world than making movies. Making movies is the hardest thing in the world. I think when people say like, "It's not brain surgery." Yeah, it's brain surgery. It is really difficult and it's leading a team of people into battle against time and it is a bit of a Hercules task and I would never do it unless I'm passionate. It doesn't make sense because otherwise get a day job. You'd probably make more money and it will be more consistent and you won't be you know watching your back every five seconds. With film making it's really; it's not easy, but it's rewarding. If you're doing it because you love what you're doing and you know what dude, no matter what anybody has ever said about *Jason Goes to Hell* — I love that movie. That's my baby and I did it because I wanted a career and I wanted a career in horror movies and it gave me that.

CLIMAX

Looking back on these interviews, I consider myself both lucky and torn. I've interviewed some great names in some of the most influential franchises in cinematic history. As nice as it would be to say that I've reached some great conclusion and analysis of them all: I haven't. What I do know is that the majority of these people are inspired, and go forward, due to their dedication to creating something great.

Each time I reach a consensus with these interviews, another one makes me think in a different way. Jeff Burr, Adam Marcus and Peter Webber, to name just a few of them, obviously care about what they do, put high levels of details into their films and truly care about their creations. I wouldn't say Uwe Boll doesn't care about his films but he certainly has the fiscal awareness that lots of people don't openly discuss in creation with their art.

Does Kevin Yagher not directing anymore due to a bad studio experience mean he doesn't care about films? Of course not, these are all individuals with backstories and contexts that affect their decisions. It might be that I'm too close to them to actually see it. For you, it may be easier to see the things that separate and divide them.

It seems like legacy is something that matters to everyone, however. I was struck by Adam Marcus' telling of how he was told to get rid of the hockey mask, and the clip he refers to on YouTube shows Cunningham firmly deny that it was his decision, but it does make a lot more sense that it would be. Also, as far as I'm concerned, what does Adam Marcus have to gain from telling that story so many years on, what would it change?

Some fans love that film, others don't, that's the nature of the beast, but he's clearly smart enough to understand that telling that lie wouldn't rewrite his career or change the final product, but for Cunningham it might.

I know I'm no Harper Lee and can quit writing just because I've written one book, and I'm far too unimportant for a lawyer to screw me out of one when I'm ill, too.

Stephen King talks about how he was labelled the horror guy and took it as a compliment, but I'm unsure if I want to be defined by something like that across my career.

Ideally, it will span decades and my tastes and style will grow and not be similar across. Peter Webber directed *Girl with a Pearl Earring* four years before *Hannibal Rising*, and since then hasn't done a feature film that bears a resemblance. Uwe Boll, despite being known for his multiple adaptations of video games, directed films of his own ideas that received positive reviews. Perhaps this does go to show that people, myself included, do cling to these marketable labels. Actually, many of these directors are not purely horror directors, but have gone on to make successful films outside of the genre.

I found a way to work against how much I procrastinate.

Rather than nap the day away and rack up hundreds of hours on video games, I've found that having a to-do list means that I can work toward end goals, albeit it does take out some of the romanticism of creating art.

Here's what a standard day looks like for me when I'm in the flow, depending on whether I'm working and how far along I am:

1. Take Medications

2. Shower and Shave

3. Go to Work

4. Read X amount of Pages

5. Write X words.

Of course, that list is always longer with more mundane things like go to the bank or pick up socks, things that are hardly worth sharing as if they belong on the stone tablets for Moses to share with the world. The first three are easily accomplished too, I have to show up and stand somewhere, but it does mean it's done, and I'm building momentum. It's that same momentum, too that means by reading and writing a certain amount of day things can get done. It's not as if anyone in this book just sits idly by waiting for the phone to ring, they pitch and go out and work day to day and if you looked at artists and creators as a per hour wage for the amount of time they put in, it would be one of the lowest paying jobs on the planet.

The thing is, I do believe art is a skill that can be refined and developed as time goes on. Considering that I don't have to work with others to the same level that directors do, I think it's fair to say that my vision will be compromised less by others, which means that the only person I truly have to hold accountable is myself. There isn't much else to say other than the road is long and I will walk through it and sometimes it will be difficult and unrewarding until there are those moments, something as simple as a perfect sentence, where it'll all be worth it.

One of the most beautiful moments about this journey, is how much these directors value their fans, and then the fans still care for these movies and characters, too. Think of those people, the people that might be us, the people we might be worried about talking to while stuck at a party, the person who watches all those specific and odd films and can make you a top 10 list of a franchise that you've never heard of. These are the loyal people who don't just follow trends but follow artists more than the general public, who will buy the DVDs rather than just stream online and keep people in work and giving them the option to continue to create. If I had one person who was 1/10th dedicated to me as the multitude of people who are loyal to them, I'd be happy with what I was doing.

The people who have been featured in this book are all role models, in one shape or form, to me. They took the leap forward to create, and that's something that not as many people can say as they'd like. It's easy to dream of doing something artistic, and nothing wrong with never pursuing it, but these people got behind the camera and created something for others. Regardless of the result, they made something for the fans as well as themselves, and that's more than a lot of people can say. Some of them wouldn't want to repeat the experience and look back on the final product with distain, but it's still something brave that other people can appreciate. Ultimately, they are some of the people who founded Sequelland, but they never moved out of it, it's a permanent address with no way to take it back. At least they're aware of it, and tried to make it their own.

INTERVIEW WITH JEFF BURR

"I mean it's looking at it in a rearview mirror; the road doesn't look so good. But travelling over the road, it wasn't so bumpy."

Selected Filmography:

From A Whisper To A Scream
Stepfather II
The Texas Chainsaw Massacre III
Puppet Master 4
Puppet Master 5: The Final Chapter
Pumpkinhead II: Blood Wings

Did you always mean to go into primarily horror after your first feature being a drama?

Well, I mean, it's something I always loved. Any director will tell you, I think, any director will tell you that he would not want to be pigeonholed into one type of movie, but in other words, I love horror films, but I also love Jerry Lewis films, you know what I mean?

So did I anticipate that when I first started that the bulk of my filmmaking career so far would be in horror? No. But I love it. There are worse things that could happen as a filmmaker.

When you made *From a Whisper to a Scream*, was it less common back then to do an anthology film?

I would say, certainly, like any sub-genre, it has sits and starts and certainly, there were less anthologies made then than there are in the last five years here, but the *Twilight Zone* movie had come out and *Creepshow,* and so there were a few antecedents that were fairly current, but there weren't that many anthologies. I mean, there were, by the time we ended up coming out, there was like *Creepshow* 2 and *Deadtime Stories* and *Nightmares*, which was a kind of a failed TV pilot they ended up putting out theatrically.

So there definitely were some anthologies in the mix, it wasn't like now where there's just so many of them, you know?

After that you got *Stepfather II*?

And with that, for sure looking over my filmography, I'm sure you can ascertain there wasn't any kind of career strategy that was undertaken. So it was like what was available, you would have your own private project, try to get it made, and then you would have to make a living.

And the other thing, when your first movie is not—it was certainly successful in many ways, just on a personal level and career level for me, but it certainly was not a hit. And it was not perceived in the industry as anything approaching a hit. So when your first movie is not a hit, and no one really, you know, no one jumps up and says, "I've got to champion this movie."

Then the second movie and the third movie are that much harder to get made, or to get employed, quite frankly.

And I was so naive that I thought, *okay*, after I made the first movie, *oh for sure, I will do a second, third, fourth. It's just—of course*, you know? And it's not the case at all. If you make an independent first movie, the cinema graveyard is filled with people that made one movie and that was it.

So I feel very lucky and blessed on some level to have had a chance to make a second movie, a second feature. So *Stepfather II* came as a direct result of *From a Whisper to a Scream* in and indirect way.

The head of foreign distribution at ITC had seen *From a Whisper to a Scream* for possible distribution. He turned it down, but he always remembered us, I guess, and my brother had met him when he was producing it to print, and they had a good conversation. So, I guess we were in his mind, and when ITC decided to make a low-budget sequel to a successful movie of theirs called, *The Stepfather*, he remembered us and called us out of the blue.

It picked up a lot of steam, with the original actors returning and the Weinsteins involved.

But they were involved much later because it was totally financed and made by ITC, and it was originally made for a new division that would just deal with low-budget sequels and directly to video market. So it was supposed to come out April of 1989, direct to video. That's exactly what was supposed to happen and what happened was when they saw the movie starting to be put together, they thought it was,

"Hey, we might be able to get a theatrical on this" and so they saw a theatrical release, and so they partnered with the Weinsteins and, or sold it to them outright—I'm not even sure how that worked, but so then very late in the game, after the movie was completely finished; and by completely finished I mean, completely finished, the negative cut, everything. The Weinsteins got involved and they wanted to make it a little more, so called, *horrific*, or whatever; a little more gore, whatever. So they spent some money. I don't know how much they spent. Maybe they spent 30 grand, 40 grand to do a few little things, which ultimately meant nothing. And I wish they'd come to me and said, "We have 30 grand. We want to spend it on this movie, how would you improve it?" I would've loved that. And so the reason I say that is by no means did I think it was a ways perfect movie or anything, but we did the best we could at the time with the money involved, you know?

The big thing was we pushed for it; we've got to get Terry O'Quinn back...

And it sounds very, "Oh. Of course", but it wasn't the case at all. They were prepared to make the movie without him, and we just really fought and fought and fought and said, "You've got to get this guy. I mean there's nobody else that can play him."

The bar, that I could see, was pretty low when they hired us to do the movie because their expectations were *we're just going to crank this thing out and throw it direct to video, and it's going to make "x" amount of dollars. We calculated how much money it will make,* all that kind of thing. So we raised the bar for them, at least, however we did, we made them think bigger, you know, even though it was a much cheaper movie than the original *Stepfather*.

When you know it's on track to get a direct DVD

release, it must be pretty thrilling to know that then you're getting a wide theatrical one.

For me, it wasn't thrilling at all because as a director, because I had finished the movie, and had fought all the battles and everything else, and then all of a sudden, I've got to fight all these battles again; because now another company has bought it and they have their own ideas. And the Weinsteins were known for being very... you know the classic example a fireman who's an arsonist so then it can look like a hero by putting out fires.

One of our big victories, if you will, in terms of the franchise is that we got Terry to do it again. That's the main reason why it worked. And you can make a case that number two's are really the crutch, because that's either at the end of it all or the beginning of a real franchise. You know there's a process because if you don't do a good job or if it doesn't work, then that's the end of it, one *and* two. So you can hardly call that a franchise. But if it all works, you might have a third, fourth, a remake, whatever, you know? So, I'm proud of the contribution I made to that series, and Terry was just a wonderful person to work with. I can't begin to tell you how wonderful he was; and generous, and everything else.

Yeah. It was just a great experience to be able to work with him. It was actually a hit on a moderate level, and I don't know really know if it really did it propel my career in any way, really? I don't know. But I don't know if I would have gotten *Chainsaw* if I hadn't done that.

It's interesting that you were saying that two is kind of the crux of a franchise, and then with *Chainsaw*, you did join for the third one.

Yes. And that was a very odd for many reasons. I came in at

the last minute. I would say I had very little development of the script time. If somebody had come to me and said, "Hey, we want to make a third *Chainsaw* movie, that would not have been the movie I would have made; script wise, I would say. It's just that would not have been the direction I would've taken.

Was it difficult joining the franchise considering it has two entries already, compared to when you did *Stepfather*, which had only one?

Yeah. And I didn't really think like that, and really, with *Chainsaw*, I did feel obligated to Tobe Hooper, just as I felt obligated to Joe Ruben, because you're building on the foundation they've already built.

And you don't want to *wreck the house*, you know, so to speak. The second one was so, for most people, wacky and out of tone with what they expected, that it almost felt like a whole different movie. It didn't feel like a *Chainsaw* movie, at least in a lot of people's minds.

Was there studio interference from people who weren't involved in the process?

Oh, God, oh. Studio interference, well, yeah. That's part and parcel with getting hired to do something with very little experience, but in particular, that movie was difficult because I didn't have my brother and Darin Scott wasn't producing it, so I was kind of the lone voice in the wilderness. I felt all the other producing people were people that worked for New Line or people that had worked for New Line.

It's just, like, you spend so much time defending or arguing your creative decisions, when a lot of it is very intuitive and unexplainable and to have a guy who's completely non-creative asking over and over again, "Well, why do you want to do it this way? Why do you want to do it this way?" It's horrendous.

So I can't say I was supported. But looking back on it, I don't know why I would've ever thought I would've been supported, I knew I wasn't the first choice. And I guess I didn't realize how far down the totem pole I was because some people turned that movie down for a variety of reasons. And I was the first guy that, I guess, had credits good enough to satisfy their corporate idea of what a director should be, that accepted the role.

I know Peter Jackson was rumored and then it's kind of ironic that you ended up working with Viggo Mortensen.

Well, yes. I don't know if that wasn't in any way a direct connection; I don't think, but it was like Peter Jackson saw him in *Leatherface* and said, "Oh man. I love that guy."

But at the time, but I don't know if Peter Jackson was officially offered the movie, but they knew they definitely at that time wanted to work with him. A lot of directors turned it down because of the time or lack of time. I'm sure they met at least 30 other people, you know?

Was there a part of you that was delighted to contribute to a franchise? You said you liked the first *Chainsaw*.

Oh. I loved the first *Chainsaw*. I adored the first *Chainsaw*, in the sense that it is an amazing independent American movie. I mean forget horror film, forget anything else; It's just a classic, independent, American horror movie—American movie, period. As it should be when you talk about *Shadows*, when you talk about *Faces*. When you talk about Robert Young stuff, whatever, you put that there too. Put that in the mix because it's absolutely of that stature. So it's an amazing movie, and certainly, time has been very kind to it, and it's a classic, independent, American film.

And there's no way—and I knew this at the time, there's no way to ever come close to duplicating that movie on a professional, mainstream way; because this movie, *Leatherface* was a totally professional, totally mainstream movie, even though it was a low-budget movie. In other words, it was made very traditionally. It had a crew of a certain size, and that's what you couldn't fight against. It just was.

That's how they worked, and it was all that kind of stuff. So there was no way in those conditions, you could ever duplicate that movie, or even come close to anything— in terms of art direction, in terms of performance, just everything; because so much of that movie—of the first movie, is informed and infected by how it was made.

When you went into the sets of the *Puppet Master* films, was there a smaller working environment?

Well that is a whole different deal and I mean, it's going to sound harsh, but I had, just to be honest with you, I had much less respect for the *Puppet Master* franchise than the *Chainsaw* franchise or the *Stepfather*.

I was pleasantly surprised by the third movie, because that had some fun ideas and some production value and all that. So again, this was a case of basically, having to make a living in the sense that I made an independent movie before this that took about a year and a half to make and it did nothing, and so I had to turn down some other stuff in order to finish it, and all that, and it did nothing on the circuit, and it did nothing for my pocketbook or for anything, you know, for a career. But I'm still glad I made the movie.

I got a phone call out of the blue to come in for a meeting on this movie, and, these two movies, and what he offered me, *Puppet Master* was just only part of the equation. January '93, when he called me he says, "I will guarantee you will do four movies this year, and by the end of the year, you will make "x" amount of dollars, and you have four movies." And I thought, "Okay. That's something I could do." And it was *Puppet Master 4 and* 5, and *Oblivion* 1 *and* 2. down in Romania. And I love Westerns and that was great. And then for a variety of reasons, *Oblivion* 1 *and* 2 was given to another director. So, anyways, the reason I took those movies, it was part of a bigger deal, you know?

So I was aware of the franchise. As a matter of fact, I saw *Puppet Master,* the first movie at a screening before it came out. I always had a problem with the series conceptually, that if like, well, if they're kids movies, then they should be kind of kids movies, but if they're going to be R-rated horror movies, then make them much more outrageous than they are.

And I felt it was very tame for R-Rated horror movies, and it's one thing if you're going to do *The Gate* or something, okay then do *The Gate.* But if you're going to make it an R-rated movie, then add sexual components to the Puppets, or just much more imagination.

Did you have to strictly follow the lore established in the previous three films?

Well, I mean, basically, everything I said I wouldn't do again, I did. You're kind of shot out of a cannon to make them. We were doing two movies simultaneously, and so the script was like 180 pages or something, and so it was more like a miniseries kind of mentality I guess. The script, we did what we could on the set, but then it was a mess. I mean a total mess. They certainly don't fit snugly in the *Puppet Master* previous series, the previous three movies. So, I think, you just drive yourself crazy looking at that whole series with any idea of continuity and who does what and why. They're little effects set pieces that are hopefully amusing to watch and it's a great stop motion. I mean Dave Allen is really the reason that series worked, if it worked at all, because each stop motion was just wonderful.

The franchise has got 10 or 11 films made now?

I think, 10 or 11, yeah, I think. And he left after five. Five was the last one he did. And so there really wasn't stop motion in any of the other ones.

Have you watched any of the other films since?

I watched the sixth, because I knew the director and a friend of mine was in it as an actor. I got some chuckles because I thought my movies were low budget, but that was even more problematic, budgetarily. I've seen clips of the one they did in China.

In the sense that it was so quick where there was only so much you could do, in terms of the script; because the logistics were already underway, in terms of sets being built and all that. You're dealt a hand of cards and your job is to play the hand of cards as best you can, even if it's shit. Even if it's like about a mish-mash of everything, you've got to play the hand as best you can, as long as you can, you know? So that's always been my MO, anyway, just to give it your all and no sense just coming there with the attitude, "Oh. It's just going to be a piece of shit. Let's just walk through it." I mean that's just unconscionable, you got to at least try and try to squeeze every drop of lemon, to try and make lemonade, you know?

It's part of the art, or whatever. You know, painters go through it; novelists go through it, and nobody like in the movies. So you made something that you love and think, "Well, there's got to be some people that would love this, because I love it." And in that case, you know, it really was. And I'm exaggerating to make a point.

It's a love it or hate it movie and the percentage is about 10 and 90. That movie was nothing but joy to make and to develop and to everything because I did everything on that movie. So it was joyful, absolutely joyful. There's a saying—"Take the joy in the process, not the results", and that's for me, personally, that is the living embodiment of that saying.

The worst day in a movie is still an extremely enjoyable day, 'cause you love what you do, you know. It's always enjoyable on many, many levels. Especially, shooting on film, you really felt that; and I say shooting on film because there was a sense, misguided or not, there was a sense of permanence, so you felt, "Whatever I'm doing this day, these 3,000', 5,000' feet of film that I'm going to expose today, there could be that one—at least this is how I always felt. It's going to sound horribly pretentious, maybe, and I don't mean it that way, but it's just you felt, everyday there would be possibly that one image or that one moment that would stick in someone's mind, forever.

Because you've got someone who's paying you to do what you love, and I just love this. Almost all these sets are fascinating to be around because there's a mixture of just fascinating people. I mean some out of their minds, some just low key and incredibly smart, whatever. There's just always a mix of incredibly interesting people.

You went into another franchise, right?

Well, again, not intentionally or anything.

But, yeah. That's what happened. I had no career or strategies; and that was probably a huge mistake, because if I had a career or strategy as to where—I hate this term—so called building and brand and whatever, from the beginning, you would never do as many sequels as I did. Because even to be known as *the sequel guy* I mean, what kinda thing is that to be known for? I mean, you're a parasite, you know, so I did them because I love making movies. It's an addiction, and I was an addict; I still am, in the sense of the experience of making a movie is always valuable because we learn. So that was my mindset, I *will learn on every movie, so I want to do as many movies as I can*, and as I say, as a career strategist, you would never do that, you know?

I have no one to blame or to say I got fucked over, because I totally made those choices, and those choices were such that once I reached, probably, my mid-thirties, they're going, "This guy's is—", you know, 'cause nobody really looks inside the movie. They just look at the filmography on IMDB or whatever.

So they don't really examine the movies and the situations the movies were made under, and so they look at me and go, "Okay. This guy doesn't care and he'll do whatever", you know, and nobody cares about his movies, in the end; onto the next. So that's something I have had to struggle against, in subsequent years, and so, you know, I am very happy with some of the stuff I did in the sense of it really formed who I am as a filmmaker and all that. Look at my filmography. When I was at USC, if I had seen my filmography, now in my early fifties, I would go, "Oh, this guy sucks."

You know, and again, judge nothing on the arrogance of youth. I would just be looking at the set thinking, "I will never be this guy." It goes part and parcel with making a lot of sequels, I think, the identity is always going to be someone else's.

I mean it's looking at it in a rear view mirror; the road doesn't look so good. But traveling over the road, it wasn't so bumpy.

And presumably, while that was happening, all these other meetings begin.

I was also trying to get my own projects going, and some of the other stuff I was trying to get going were very strange. Things that you would have to be David Lynch to believe to do it and to get financing. I was always trying to do other stuff, but at the end of the day, and as I say, this is my mind-set, I'd rather be making a movie than not making a movie.

And that's not the greatest attitude if you want to build a brand.

Why is it do you think that horror sequels happen more than any other film genre?

Well, economics. Most horror films in the 80's and 90's were low-budget studio movies. So doing a sequel, it was just a pure economic thing. You had a loyal audience and you could do a sequel for ½ or ¼ of the original project, and it'll come out with that name, and it will do "x" amount of business. And it's still that way. I mean, because horror fans; I count myself in this league—they are an incredibly loyal audience.

And incredibly obsessive in many ways, and a lot of them are completists, and even if they know *Hellraiser 12* is going to suck, they'll watch it because it's *Hellraiser 12*...

Nothing against the *Hellraiser* groups. It's just some people are like that. And if you have an iconic character, a James Bond, that can be re-invented throughout the years, that leads to a soil that is rich to plant as many sequels as you want, you know?

Like *Friday the 13th*. The first time I saw it was on Halloween. The first time I saw *Halloween*, in 1979, did I think or even imagine a sequel to *Halloween* when I saw it?

Hell, no! Absolutely not! It was a perfectly contained, self-contained movie, but now you would probably think about sequels. Like a young audience now, they would go, "Okay. I can't wait for the next one." So people have that mentality that there's no such thing as a self-contained movie anymore. Certainly not a self-contained genre movie, because there's always going to be room left for the audience to go, "Okay. I can't wait for the next one, and the next one", you know; which is ludicrous. I hate that, because the first James Bond movie, the first *Halloween*, *Night of the Living Dead,* I mean if you're going to do a sequel—you see *Night of the Living Dead* lent itself to a sequel.

And the sequel wasn't any direct sequel, per se, but it was in the same world. And that's the way to do it. If you create a world that can then be re-interpreted, whatever, great.

But just to do, you know, *Friday the 13th 2, 3, 4*, et cetera, I mean, ultimately, I just never understood it, whichever way you're coming from, a guy with my filmography, I never would've believed. If you told me in '79 there's gonna be, how many *Halloween* movies, it's just unbelievable, really. So I think horror movies, because of the economics i.e. lower-budget movies usually, and they're not star driven. That's a key. Traditionally, they're not star driven, where if they're a star-driven movie to do a sequel, that actor's gonna demand more money, if it hasn't been locked in, yet. Whereas in horror films, that really never happens, because it's almost exclusively not actor driven. They're makeup driven. They're filmmaker driven, for sure. In other words, they're the one genre, one of the only genres, if not the only genre to have a completely unknown cast.

It is usually an asset because then you don't know the billing pecking order of who's going to live who's going to die; 'cause you don't know any of them.

But if you saw Bruce Willis, Benedict Cumberbatch, whatever, if you saw him, you know he is not going to die in reel one. It's one of the only genres where it helps you to have an unknown cast and it helps you to have raw production value.

Do you think lots of the directors that join these kinds of long running franchises get in at the last minute, the same way that you did in some of those films?

I think it's a great, even now, it's a great learning experience to do a first movie, because also there's that, if there's ever a guarantee or anything, which there isn't, but it's a good learning experience whereas for someone to hire an unknown director, because whatever they do, they're, it's still going to make "x" amount of dollars, even if they completely fuck it up, it's still going to make "x" amount of dollars. The problem now, and what I just said harkens back to the '80s and '90s, now it's really not that way.

There's no such thing as *Friday the 13th franchise* where they may have put a known director on it or something, because every movie's got to be a home run; that's the actual movie.

Every movie is made with the intention that it's got to be a huge, huge hit, in a marketing juggernaut that will spawn amusement park rides and all that shit. So it really isn't, even *Paranormal Activity* 2, 3 that got just as much expectation in weight as *Jurassic World* on some executive world.

Is there anything else you'd like to say looking back on your career?

One thing I just want to emphasize, the need to talk to the original directors, and I had a great conversation with Joe Ruben when I did *Stepfather* 2, very illuminating, very funny. Then I was told that I couldn't talk to Tobe Hooper legally for whatever crazy, New Line reason, but I ended up talking to him after the fact. I have seen him on and off over the years, and he's nothing but gracious to me. And then I did meet Stan Winston, who I was forbidden to talk to, too because of because of the legal thing, and so I met him at Stitches, Film Festival in Spain, and he was in the bar alone. I think he had just gotten in, and I was walking by and I happened to see him; I knew what he looked like. So I went up to introduce myself, "Ah, Mr. Winston, I'm a big fan of your work, blah, blah, blah" A friend of mine was your production side-arm on *Pumpkinhead,* blah, blah, blah. And as a matter of fact, I directed *Pumpkinhead* 2.

He turned around—almost apologetically as I said it, you know? Because I knew he did not want that movie to be made. He actively did not want that movie being made. And so he just kind of looked at me, more like scowled at me and left. He didn't say a word. So I was wondering, "Did he hear me? Because he could've been jet lagged. Or maybe he just hated me on sight because I directed it, poking it through, I don't know. But the other thing, is I say it kiddingly, but I think it's true. I never killed off his franchise.

So I feel proud of that.

Well you never had the last word with the franchise either, so, a doubled edged sword.

Yeah. There must be plenty of those in the industry.

INTERVIEW WITH JOHN SKIPP

"There is no escape from the horror of horror."

Filmography:

A Nightmare on the Elm Street 5: The Dream Child
Tales of Halloween
Monsterland

You are a screenwriter and a prose writer. Do you know when a story will be better for the screen or for the page?

Funny thing is, I'm a cinematic prose writer, and always have been. So *whatever* I'm writing, I'm pretty much experiencing the movie in my mind from the inside. From there, it generally comes down to whether I think I'll get to direct the movie or not. If it's a movie I want to make, I'll probably do the screenplay first. Then, if that doesn't work, I might just make a book or short story out of it.

JAKE'S WAKE (with Cody Goodfellow) and *THE LONG LAST CALL* both started as scripts, which were then adapted to prose form. My short story "*Art is the Devil*" was the same deal, originally intended as a short segment of an anthology film that never got made. Sometimes the story's just too good to be left to die. Either write it as prose, or it will probably be lost forever.

I'm going through a very similar but much more expansive process right now with Autumn Christian on a book called *RIKKI RAGE*, which started as a screenplay with Cody but then mushroomed and transmogrified into a wildly different (and better) novel. If this book were turned into a film, the script would have to be almost entirely rewritten.

On the same note, my book *CONSCIENCE* really wanted to be a screenplay, but it just wouldn't come. Banged on it for months, but nothing. Then one day, I walked into the legendary bookstore Dark Delicacies, saw all the books that came out since the last time I'd written one, and thought, "Hey! It might be fun to do one of those again." Then went home and, within two hours, wrote the first chapter. And six weeks later, the book was done.

In an unlikely arc of completion, I've just been hired to adapt *CONSCIENCE* into a screenplay. Which makes me insanely happy.

The thing is, they're different disciplines. Compared to actual prose, screenplays are like haiku. More to the point, they are blueprints for the film, which hardly anyone will ever read. They're also far more fragile, in that they can be taken away from you and rendered unrecognizable. Whereas with a book, nobody fucks with you. Your words are your own.

And here's the last thing about that. When you write a script, you are providing instructions for the director, the producers, actors, the director of photography, the production designer, the special fx artists, the location scouts, the stunt people, the composer, not to mention wardrobe, hair, and all the way down the line. Then they will take that shit and run.

But in a novel, you ARE the director, the actors, the director of photography, and everyone else. You have to provide all the sensations, using nothing but words. It's a much harder job than screenwriting, just in terms of sheer labor. But the trick is, writing scripts only really gets hard when you want to write them well, not just squeeze 'em out for a buck.

What was the experience working on an established horror property like Nightmare on *Elm Street?*

I mean, it started out fun. As it turns out, producer Mike De Luca was a huge fan of our book *THE LIGHT AT THE END*, and the emerging splatterpunk scene in general. So New Line Cinema conducted a splatterpunk cattle call, in which a bunch of writers were called in to pitch their ideas. And Spector and I won. But we then had two weeks to write it. So we hammered out a draft that mapped out the whole story and mythology in great detail. It was very dark, and metaphysically layered. Explaining "The Dream Pool" of the collective unconscious, and Freddy as a toxic oil spill within it, which is how he leaks into your head while you sleep. Amping the whole "bastard son of a thousand maniacs" thing, and showing how he was raised by cruel nuns, and that's what turned him into a monster. All kinds of cool stuff.

To be fair, we concentrated a lot harder on the story architecture than we did on the dialogue. So the script wasn't perfect yet. Ostensibly, that's what second drafts are for.

But as it turns out, they had another writer they liked, writing their own version of *THE DREAM CHILD*. (Which isn't technically legal, but what the hey.) He turned in his script. We turned in ours. They hated his, and were excited by ours. So they promptly fired us, and hired him to rewrite ours.

Hilariously, their big note was, "This is like if Stanley Kubrick made an *Elm St.* film." And we said, "Cool, huh?" And they said, "No." Next thing we knew, we were out the fucking door. (laughs)

Honestly, it was the single shittiest experience of my professional career. (laughs) I'm not kidding. Kinda like *THE HUMAN CENTIPEDE,* only with less dignity, as the producers rammed one writer after another face-first up each other's asses. Six writers and thirteen drafts later, they had the piece-of-shit movie they evidently wanted. And then – because Spector and I came up with the original story and wrote the first draft – we had to threaten them with legal action to get our names on the credits.

I talk about this extensively on the documentary *NEVER SLEEP AGAIN: THE ELM ST. LEGACY*. And I can

honestly say that the only really good thing to come out of the experience was meeting Andrew Kasch, who co-directed that doc, and with whom I've made movies off-and-on ever since.

What keeps you going back to the page?

I genuinely love writing. Not just making up stories, but the process of writing. Inhabiting the stories. Inhabiting the characters. Again, dreaming it all from the inside. It's an enormous pleasure. And the longer I do it, the more honed my skills. So I'm always trying new shit, posing new challenges. Like climbing the Himalayas, only without the stupid plummeting- to-your-death part.

Do you have any rituals when writing?

Oh, yeah. I generally designate three-to-five hours daily to the actual writing. When it's time to sit down, I pop my first beer, light my first cigarette, spark up a joint, and go to town. It's like the curtain opens, and IT'S SHOWTIME, FOLKS! Then I party with my story till I fucking drop. And I do this every single day. That's how I keep it lively and fun.

You wrote the novelization for *Fright Night*, what's it like doing this adaptation of licensed property?

It was a fun challenge, very early in my career. Spector and I were given a chunk of cash and one month to pull it off. We got Columbia Pictures to send us some stills from the film (which had already been shot), and were greatly inspired by the phenomenal makeup and effects. We also had a quick phone conversation with writer/director Tom Holland, who has since become a friend. (He actually appears as "The Clown With No Name" in my short film *CLOWNTOWN*, co-directed with Andrew Kasch, from a script by Cody Goodfellow. And he's terrific.)

It was also notable in that it was the first time Spector had to buy a typewriter and leap into the actual writing fray. (He was involved with every speck of story in *THE LIGHT AT THE END*, and actually came up with the idea, but I did 99.9% of the writing.) It was a great education, all the way around. Always fun to learn while you earn!

You have done plenty of collaborations in the past when writing, do you enjoy the process of

working from someone else, and is it better than the multiple people involved in film production?

I looooove collaborating. It comes from playing in bands as a teenager and beyond. Just the idea of having someone to play with, bounce ideas back and forth with, makes it so much more fun than doing it all yourself. Honestly, being a writer largely means sitting alone in a room for the rest of your fucking life. If you're working with the right people, it can make the world a far happier place.

That said, there's nothing worse than a bad collaboration. And that's where it can get tricky with film. When I'm producing and directing, I get to pick who I work with. Andrew and I have always designated our sets "no-asshole zones". And by and large, we've succeeded.

But when the wrong hands try to stick their spoons in your soup, it can get ugly. That's why I rarely want to be involved with films where I'm not directing, or don't trust the people in charge 100%. Otherwise, it's a recipe for hell. (See *NIGHTMARE* 5, above.) I'd rather work in a fucking gas station than get pushed around by people who don't care, are only in it for the money.

That said, I've worked with some wonderful producers who really do care. And I love actors. And I love crew. Have sooooo much respect for people who love their jobs, play well with others, and take care to perfect their skills. A well-run movie set is my favorite playground in the world.

In the day of remakes, reboots and sequels what do you find refreshing?

I am continually inspired by original, idiosyncratic one-of-a-kind artists, doing work that nobody else could have done. That's the shit I love. That's the shit I do. Bottom line: I don't follow trends. Trends follow me. And that's how I like my artists.

Right now, in film, there are many fresh voices I admire like Justin Benson and Aaron Moorhead, Ana Lily Amirpour, David Robert Mitchell, Jeremy Saulnier, Jennifer Kent, Jenn Wexler, and Ari Aster. My two favorite movies of 2018 were *SORRY TO BOTHER YOU* by Boots Riley and *BORDER* by Ali Abassi. You've never seen two more jaw-droppingly original movies in your life.

I'm incredibly excited by the Etheria Film Night's roster of extraordinary female genre filmmakers. That's how I discovered quite a few of my new favorites like Laura Moss, Stephanie Cabdevila, Gigi Saul Guerrero, and many many more. Have no doubt these women are gonna change the game in many significant, magnificent ways.

And then, of course, I always go back to my favorites: George Romero, The Coen Brothers, Preston Sturges, Stanley Kubrick, Russ Meyer, David Cronenberg, Hal Ashby, Juzo Itami, Alejandro Jodorowsky, David Lynch, Seijun Suzuki, Quentin Tarantino, Guy Madden, Takashi Miike. The list goes on and on. But what they all have in common is that nobody else could do what they do. And that's all that I ask.

You've had a long career that's featured successful films, million copy selling books, successful anthologies and publishing fantastic works of fiction— how is it in retrospective for yourself?

You mean, how do I look back at the body of my work? I'm mostly really happy. As a matter of fact, *NIGHTMARE* 5 is one of the only things I'm *not* proud of! But then I can point at *TALES OF HALLOWEEN* – a meatgrinder of a production with a two-day shoot that was also almost stupifyingly fun, with an incredible cast and crew – and go, "Okay, now that one I'm cool with!"

Honestly, my only real regret at this point is that I haven't made more movies. But rumour has it, *that's what we get whole lives for!* (laughs) So definitely looking forward to that.

If you had an unlimited budget what would your dream passion project be, in and out of established franchises?

If I had an unlimited budget, my passion project would be to create a slate of 10 or so original modestly-budgeted feature films and shoot them, one after another, for the rest of my life. I would most assuredly not want to squirt it all out in one place.

I believe you're creating a book about bizarre films. Why do you think horror and the surreal often go together so well?

Heather Drain and I will be releasing *THE BIZARRO ENCY- CLOPEDIA OF FILM* (*VOL. I*). And believe me, the horror section is huge, because horror is largely made out of weirdness, and any weirdness that isn't hilarious is probably horrific, or at least disturbing. I'd say they were two great tastes that taste great together, but oftentimes, *they're the exact same taste!*

How difficult do you think it is to get to be known for your own voice after working on a sequel?

I always had my own voice. The only thing working on that sequel did was kick me in the balls, send me occasional checks, and get me doing interviews like this! (laughs)

RESOLUTION

FADE IN:

Over three years ago I was doing an internship for a digital media company, skipping the last year of my undergraduate degree, then coming home and drinking and watching horror movies. I already had my first book out and I was shopping around a novel that never found a home. The amount of free time I had as a student, combined with my daydreaming and ambition to create another book, I decided to track down directors of sequels to horror movies to see if I could ask them how they felt about their careers, and learn a little about myself on the way. I tracked them down through email addresses on archived sites, Facebook, Twitter, emailing production companies and asking friends of friends if they knew anyone who would be a good fit.

It all started at a time where I didn't know what I was doing with my own life. Eventually I'd pursue postgraduate studies and spend longer focusing on my writing, but at that point I was unsure if it was time to go into work, what I wanted to do for work, and how I'd manage to focus on my dreams of becoming a writer that made important work that connected with people.

JAY SLAYTON-JOSLIN sips from a cup of coffee on his desk, puts it back down. He writes the word fuck three times on his laptop and deletes it.

The thing about creating is it takes a level of humility and drive. This, as my second book, won't define me, but it will also influence the direction that I'm going in artistically, too. I purposely haven't published another poetry collection because I don't want to be known as a poet, ideally after that there would have been a short story collection, or a novel or novella, but I'm thrilled this is the second book that has my name on it. The thing is though, it isn't easy, otherwise I wouldn't have left it six years between publication. If I look back on my bibliography now it reads *Kicking Prose* (2014), *Sequelland: A Story of Dreams and Screams* (2020). It's also misrepresentative, because I didn't spend five years at the grindstone of my laptop everyday. I studied more, travelled, fell in love, had some of the best and worst days of my life, and it all accumulated here, in each and every word.

When I started out writing, I was worried that each published story and book would define me. In a sense, people are remembered for their best (or worst) work, but what I realised through speaking to all these directors and looking at their work is that it is the one that comes after that can change it. If I wrote about horror sequels and films for the rest of my life, yeah that's fair enough to have me pegged as the horror guy, who released some poetry when he was young and then wouldn't shut up about slashers and sequels. Ernie Barbarash is a good example of this, producing and then directing a sequel, and now is doing Netflix romantic comedies. James Wan, of *Saw* and *Insidious* fame, has gone on to direct action and superhero films, and while lots of the residents of *Sequelland* have just done horror, they understand and love films or all genres, and understand the role that those films played in their own development.

Jay thinks back to his own childhood, smiling at all the things he wanted to be when he grew up.

Perhaps another reason why I grew to love sequels and franchises so much, is that I didn't read much as a child. I watched worlds form in video games and films, so would often have to wait years for new installments rather than being able to dive into something that always existed. Growing up I wanted to be a director, a samurai, a guitarist, now, I just want to be happy and create art and live a comfortable life. For me, that's primarily based around living well and focusing on creating art, and those are both things that are predominantly in my control. Of course, I'd love for the things I create to be published and received well. Who doesn't dream of dog eared pages and strangers emailing you out of the blue to thank you? It's easy to say you don't want the validation of others, but I think it's natural to understand that I do, at least a little bit.

Jay thinks about life as an old man, sitting by a fire- place in a post-apocalyptic Brexit Britain, burning copies of his books just to keep warm.

When I look back on myself in the future, I want it to be something that makes me smile, rather than wince. Of course, this is easy to say now, and I'm not expecting that path to be easy to take, nor am I expecting every decision to go in my favour and not to be disappointed. I think, though, if I take the time to create my art well, and know that it's the best that I can do at that moment, there's not much more that I can do. I'm sure in 10-year's-time, if I was to look back at this book, there would be things I'd want to change. I'm sure even before publication I'll go through it again, tear out some stuff and put it back in. Hindsight is indeed powerful, and perhaps with the greatness that it can offer, it may be so daunting to consider how we look back at the work that we create in the future, that we shouldn't spend too long on it, as it would halt the process. If Vonnegut can rank all his works like a report card and admit some were better than others, then I'm sure we can be comfortable creating what we can at the time, and as long as we are sincere and work our hardest, then we can look back and understand.

Jay opens a beer and pours it into the glass, discarding the empty and knocking over an alcoholic dominoes trail of liquor.

But it will be difficult, and that's fine. To work in solitude and for little money, to spend so much time on something that may be forgotten. It's the risk we make, though. The directors in this book still make that risk, and theirs is an even higher stake as the amount of money that goes into those films needs to see a return, and they'll be bearing the stigma if it doesn't when they go looking for future work. This isn't to suggest that any artist shouldn't be held accountable for what they create, or that audiences should back off if they don't like things or go wrong, but to simply suggest that few creators are sitting on a gold throne, and are impervious to damage or want to create something to disappoint people. All of the directors I interviewed have brought thousands of people joy through their creations, and that makes this chaotic future seem a little less scary. Especially considering so many of them were inspired by the same choices as a kid, and will go on to inspire so many others on the path that they have taken—a bloody full circle.

Jay ominously stares out into the distance, wondering if this is the end.

This is the end, for now. It all feels cathartic, I now understand what I want to do with my own process and how I want to live the rest of my life in regards to creating art. Now I understand the type of work I uncompromisingly want to create, and that I want it to connect with people, too. I think that is similar to lots of the people in this book, and they connected with me, if that means anything to them. As streaming takes over and sequels are shown to be profitable, as reboots come of franchises that we grew up on, there will be more and more entries to enrich (and distaste) what we know. If I had the wisdom and careers of these directors, and I was looking back on their filmographies as my own, I'd be happy, and I hope one day someone says the same about the field of work I plan to create in my lifetime. Until then, it's creating something for them to enjoy, so they can feel that same excitement.

FADE OUT

ACKNOWLEDGMENTS

This book wouldn't have been possible without so many people, and the impact and gratitude I feel is more so than I know how to express with words. A huge amount of credit goes to Leza and Christoph for championing this book and constantly pushing me in the right direction whenever I went off course, it's crazy how the first time we met the paperwork was signed and we were drinking and smoking cigarettes just outside of Barcelona. Distance knows no bounds with passion but it is that much sweeter when you can watch the sun go down with someone as you talk about what you love.

Furthermore thanks (and fulfilling drunken promises) to: Michael Kazepis, Pablo D'Stair, my family, Steve Rose, Chris Birt, Bradley Sands, Stephen Graham Jones, every dog in the world that lets me pet it, Gregory Howard, Sunniva Midtskogen, James Webster, Hugo Cabeza, The class of MA Writers at the University of Surrey, Judith Popova and the kind people of The Arch Bar.

Lastly, more than I can ever truly say, to my brother Jack. I don't say it much but maybe saying it here will be at least one more time - I love you. I remember the time when we were both young and I'd ask you what you are reading and you would say to me "A book of essays," and I'd say it back in a mimicking tone. Well, here you go, hold this page open and let me say it: What are you reading?

ABOUT THE AUTHOR

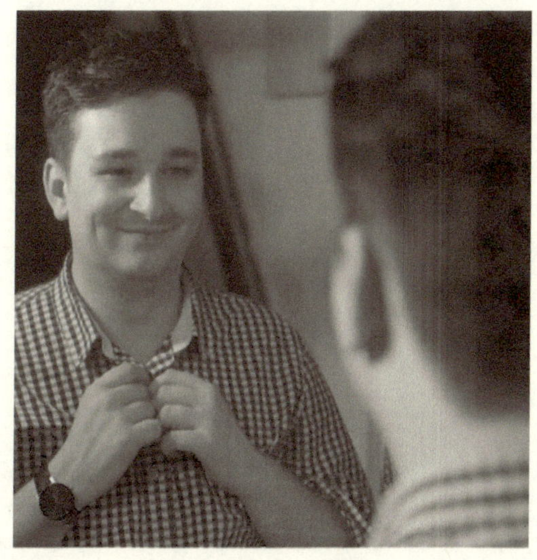

Jay Slayton-Joslin is the author of Kicking Prose (KUBOA, 2014) and Sequelland (CLASH Books, 2020). He lives in Leeds, England.

ALSO BY CLASH BOOKS

GIRL LIKE A BOMB

Autumn Christian

THIS IS A HORROR BOOK

Charles Austin Muir

TRY NOT TO THINK BAD THOUGHTS

Art by Matthew Revert

DARK MOONS RISING IN A STARLESS NIGHT

Mame Bougouma Diene

NOHO GLOAMING & THE CURIOUS CODA OF ANTHONY SANTOS

Daniel Knauf (Creator of HBO's Carnivàle)

IF YOU DIED TOMORROW I WOULD EAT YOUR CORPSE

Wrath James White

HORROR FILM POEMS

Poetry by Christoph Paul & Art by Joel Amat Güell

NIGHTMARES IN ECSTASY

Brendan Vidito

www.ingramcontent.com/pod-product-compliance
Lightning Source LLC
La Vergne TN
LVHW090951080826
845145LV00003B/967

* 9 7 8 1 9 4 4 8 6 6 7 1 6 *